Easy Grammar Grade 5 Student Workbook

Wanda C. Phillips

Easy Grammar Systems
SCOTTSDALE, ARIZONA 85255
© 2006

ALPHABETICAL LIST OF COMMONLY USED PREPOSITIONS

A

about

above

across

after

against

along

amid

among

around

at

atop

B

before

behind

below

beneath

beside

between

beyond

but (meaning except)

by

C

concerning

D

down

during

E

except

F

for

from

I

in

inside

into

L

like

N

near

O

of

off

on

onto

out

outside

over

P

past

R

regarding

S

since

T

through

throughout

to

toward

U

under

underneath

until

up

upon

W

with

within

without

A **preposition** begins a prepositional phrase. A **phrase** is a group of words. A prepositional phrase ends with a noun (something you can usually see) or pronoun (Examples: *me, him, her, us, them, you, it,* and *whom*).

Examples: The tricycle **in the backyard** is rusted.

The soccer player ran **toward me**.

Directions: Choose a preposition. Write it in the blank. Circle the prepositional phrase.

1.   She fell _____*among*_____ some sharp rocks.

    a. among

    b. over

    c. by

2.   A child crawled _____*under*_____ the table.

    a. under

    b. around

    c. onto

3.   A skunk sat _____*beside*_____ a tree.

    a. beside

    b. under

    c. behind

4.   Nicky ran _____*with*_____ her teammate.

    a. beside

    b. with

    c. behind

2

A prepositional phrase begins with a preposition. A phrase is a group of words. Therefore, a prepositional phrase is a **group of words that begins with a preposition**.

Examples: **on** the boat

after the storm

from my dad

with his aunt

behind the shed

Note that the last word is something you can see (concrete noun). Some will end in a noun such as *love* that you can't see (abstract noun). A prepositional phrase may also end with *me, him, her, us, them, you, it,* or *whom*.

ᕲᕲᕲᕲᕲᕲᕲᕲᕲᕲᕲᕲᕲᕲᕲᕲᕲᕲᕲᕲᕲᕲᕲᕲᕲᕲᕲᕲᕲᕲᕲᕲᕲᕲᕲᕲᕲᕲ

Directions: Write a preposition (that makes sense) to complete each prepositional phrase. Do not reuse any preposition.

1. _____inside_____ school

2. _____toward_____ the forest

3. _____without_____ our table

4. _____Concerning_____ a road

5. _____beside_____ his dad

6. _____behind_____ her car

7. _____regarding_____ them

8. _____with_____ your friend

9. _____atop_____ the building

10. _____amid_____ sports

11. _____past_____ their house

12. _____from_____ you

13. _____against_____ a cabin

14. _____under_____ the barber

15. _____above_____ us

16. _____near_____ the hill

3

PREPOSITIONS

Object of the Preposition

A word that ends a prepositional phrase may be a **pronoun**. A pronoun takes the place of a noun. Pronouns used frequently in prepositional phrases are *me, him, her, us, them, you, it,* and *whom*.

> Examples: Kami received tulips **from her *brother***.   (noun)
>   Kami received tulips **from *him***.   (pronoun)

Other pronouns may be used. Some examples are *none, someone, anyone, somebody, anybody,* and *any*.

> Example: Kami received tulips **from *someone***.

༄༅

Directions: In Part A, write a person's name in the blank.
              In Part B, replace the name by writing an appropriate pronoun in the blank. Write the prepositional phrase in the next blank.

> Example: A.   The email was for __**Mary**__ and __**Nikko**__.
>   (my mother's name)   (my name)
>   B.   The email was for __**us**__. __**for us**__

1. I went with my best friend to the mall.

    A.   I went **with** _Martin_ to a f̶a̶i̶r̶. *archery contest.*
                  (my best friend's name)
    B.   I went **with** _him_ to a̶ ̶f̶a̶i̶r̶. *To a archery Contest.*

2. A clown walked toward a person.

    A.   A clown walked **toward** _Molly_.
                                (your name)
    B.   A clown walked **toward** _her_. *toward her.*

3. The message was from one person and a second person.

    A.   The message was **from** _Bernadette_ and _Ronald_.
                               (a friend)   (another friend)
    B.   The message was **from** _them_. *from them*

4

A word that ends a prepositional phrase may be a **noun** or **pronoun**. This word is called the **object of a preposition**. Usually, the object of a preposition is a noun.

>Example: Leah works **with *Dan*.**   (*Dan* is a noun.)

The object of the preposition may be a pronoun.

>Example: Leah works **with *him*.**   (*Him* is a pronoun.)

തതതതതതതതതതതതതതതതതതതതതതതതതതതതതതതത

Directions: Write an appropriate object of the preposition in each space. Do not use an answer more than once. Circle the prepositional phrase.

1.   Are you eating lunch **with** _your classmate_?

2.   That woman **in the** _blue sweater_ is my neighbor.

3.   You must stay here **until** _last _____ safe_.

4.   Has Ted eaten at **that** _place on the corner_ ?

5.   Part **of her** _udder_ was swollen.

6.   My mother went to a movie **after** _the ball game_.

7.   He stepped **among some** _small rocks_ and picked up a small carton.

8.   That truck **without a** _hood_ looks odd.

9.   They leaned **against a** _mill door_ and talked.

10.   Laura sat **on an old** _stump_ while talking on her cellular telephone.

Deleting (crossing out) any prepositional phrases helps to find the subject and the verb of a sentence.

> A **prepositional phrase** begins with a preposition and ends with a noun or pronoun. A pronoun is a word like *me, him, her, us, them, you, it, whom,* or *someone*. A pronoun takes the place of a noun. A noun is something that you can usually see.

> Examples: A branch ~~of a tree~~ fell ~~during the blizzard~~.

> Marla sends stories ~~to me~~.

ฅ๏ฅ๏ฅ๏ฅ๏ฅ๏ฅ๏ฅ๏ฅ๏ฅ๏ฅ๏ฅ๏ฅ๏ฅ๏ฅ๏ฅ๏ฅ๏

Directions: Delete (cross out) any prepositional phrases. Underline the subject once and the verb twice.

1. The students gathered ~~around a telescope.~~

2. Roses bloom ~~outside my window.~~

3. Several children rolled ~~down a hill.~~

4. Joey lives ~~behind us.~~

5. Your umbrella is ~~inside the car.~~

6. Their ball rolled past ~~several toddlers.~~

7. A gray horse walked ~~toward me.~~

8. Devi crawled ~~over a white picket fence.~~

9. ~~After practice,~~ the coach talked ~~about the next game.~~

10. The teen sat ~~between his parents~~ ~~throughout the baseball game.~~

6

Directions: Delete (cross out) any prepositional phrases. Underline the subject once and the verb twice.

Example: ~~At the end of each day~~, <u>she</u> <u>jogs</u> ~~for an hour~~.

1.   This <u>subway</u> <u>winds</u> ~~through the city~~.

2.   A well-dressed <u>lady</u> <u>walked</u> ~~into a hair salon~~.

3.   One <u>carpenter</u> <u>worked</u> ~~above a doorway in the dining room~~.

4.   ~~At recess~~, two <u>boys</u> <u>played</u> ~~under an oak~~.

5.   <u>Baskets</u> ~~for dirty towels~~ <u>are</u> ~~below that open drawer~~.

6.   The <u>man</u> ~~in the black tie~~ <u>is</u> ~~from Oklahoma~~.

7.   ~~Before the track meet~~, <u>they</u> <u>sat</u> ~~near us on the grass~~.

8.   A <u>truck</u> ~~with huge tires~~ <u>backed</u> ~~into a parking space~~.

9.   A <u>stack</u> ~~of old magazines~~ <u>lay</u> ~~by the front door~~.

10.   ~~After lunch~~, the <u>ferry</u> <u>goes</u> ~~across the large lake~~.

11.   The <u>mirror</u> ~~above our long table~~ <u>fell</u> ~~without warning~~.

12.   The <u>story</u> ~~about mountain goats~~ <u>is</u> ~~beside your notebook~~.

13.   <u>Everyone</u> ~~but Jessi~~ <u>looked</u> ~~for the missing sneaker~~.

14.   <u>Mike</u> <u>placed</u> a small box ~~along an attic wall~~ and ~~between two trunks~~.

15.   ~~On every day except Sunday~~, those <u>divers</u> <u>jump</u> ~~off high cliffs~~.

A **verb phrase** is made up of at least one helping verb and a main verb. The last word in a verb phrase is called the main verb.

Verbs that can serve as helping (auxiliary) verbs are:

do	has	may	should	shall	is	were
does	have	might	would	will	am	be
did	had	must	could	can	are	being
					was	been

Sometimes, one of these serves as a main verb.

Examples: She **has** fifty cents.   main verb

She **has found** a dime.   (helping verb)   **has** + found

If the sentence is interrogative (a question), the verb phrase may be split.

Has she **found** a dime?

ஐ ஐ ஐ ஐ ஐ ஐ ஐ ஐ ஐ ஐ ஐ ஐ ஐ ஐ ஐ ஐ ஐ ஐ

Directions: Delete (cross out) any prepositional phrases. Underline the subject once and the verb or verb phrase twice. In the blank, write <u>H</u> if the italicized verb serves as a helping verb. Write <u>M</u> if the italicized verb serves as a main verb.

1.   <u>M</u>   Juan *is* ~~in the first grade~~.

2.   <u>H</u>   Juan *is* going ~~with us~~.

3.   <u>H</u>   We *have* spoken ~~with our principal~~.

4.   <u>M</u>   We *have* a note ~~from our mother~~.

5.   <u>M</u>   Grandpa *does* laundry ~~in the morning~~.

6.   <u>H</u>   *Does* your dad drive ~~to his office~~?

8

HELPING (AUXILIARY) VERBS:

do	has	may	should	shall	is	were
does	have	might	would	will	am	be
did	had	must	could	can	are	being
					was	been

A verb phrase may consist of just **one** helping verb and a main verb.

Example: **_Can_** you **drill** a hole in this piece of wood?

A verb phrase may consist of **two or more** helping verbs and a main verb.

Examples: My watch **_was broken_** for two weeks.
He **_must have been riding_** the entire afternoon.

Not is never part of a verb phrase. When you see **not** or the contraction, **n't**, in a sentence, box it immediately. Never underline it as part of a verb phrase.

Example: Jordan **did** | **_not_** | **make** his bed.

❧❧❧❧❧❧❧❧❧❧❧❧❧❧❧❧❧❧❧❧❧❧

Directions: Delete (cross out) any prepositional phrases. Underline the subject once and the verb phrase twice.

1. Mark is studying ~~for a test~~.

2. Joan has [not] hiked ~~up Camelback Mountain~~.

3. This urn must have been ~~found in Peru~~.

4. We could have driven ~~past our freeway exit~~.

5. Was your dog waiting ~~by the front door~~?

6. Her horse can be taken ~~to a nearby ranch~~.

7. [Doesn't] your neighbor build race cars ~~in his garage~~?

9

Most of the time, a prepositional phrase ends with only one word. This is called the object of the preposition.

O.P.

Example: His sister was standing on her ***head***.

Sometimes, a prepositional phrase will end with two or more words. This is called a compound object of the preposition.

O.P.   O.P.

Example: I am leaving with ***Kim*** and ***Alex***.

O.P.   O.P.   O.P.

My father is going to ***Austin***, ***Fort Worth***, or ***Dallas***.

❧❧❧❧❧❧❧❧❧❧❧❧❧❧❧❧❧❧❧❧❧❧❧❧❧

Directions: Delete any prepositional phrases. Underline the subject once and the verb/verb phrase twice. Label each object of the preposition – **O.P.**

1. Their mother makes a soup with beef and dumplings.

2. A stray dog came toward Gena and me.

3. I left without my raincoat or umbrella.

4. They will not stay at the new hotel until June or July.

5. A package from their aunt and uncle was delivered today.

6. That movie was about men and women in our fight for freedom.

7. The bag of bagels, buns, and muffins remained inside the car.

8. An article concerning sailboats and motorboats appears in this magazine.

9. We haven't seen him since Monday or Tuesday.

10

PREPOSITIONS

Compound Subject

Sometimes, a sentence will be about two or more things or people. This is called a **compound subject**.

Continue to cross out prepositional phrases so that you can find the subject and verb.

Examples: **Joan** and **I** live ~~on Byrd Street~~.

A **skateboard** and a **bike** are ~~in the driveway~~.

☙☙☙☙☙☙☙☙☙☙☙☙☙☙☙☙☙☙

Directions: Delete (cross out) any prepositional phrases. Underline the subject once and the verb twice.

1. Eggs and milk are ~~in the refrigerator~~.

2. My mom and dad departed ~~from the Orlando airport~~.

3. A robin and two cardinals flew ~~along the path~~.

4. My dog and cat run ~~through the sprinklers~~.

5. ~~For lunch~~, the boys and girls ate tacos.

6. A tape and a CD lay ~~under his bed~~.

7. Bicycles, tricycles, and skates are ~~on sale at that store~~.

8. ~~During spring break~~, Dan, Deka, and I flew ~~to Arizona~~.

9. Miss Smith and her friend turned their horses ~~toward a sloping trail~~.

10. ~~On Fridays~~, the doctor and his staff leave ~~at noon~~.

11. ~~After recess~~, the teacher and children walked ~~into their classroom~~.

12. Are peanuts and chocolate chips ~~in this dessert~~?

11

Sometimes, two or more things *happen* or *are* in a sentence. This is called a **compound verb**.

Examples: A finch **chirped** and **darted** around its cage.

The child **has** four dimes but **needs** six for cheese strips.

Continue to delete prepositional phrases so that you can find subject and verb.

ᝄ ᝄ ᝄ ᝄ ᝄ ᝄ ᝄ ᝄ ᝄ ᝄ ᝄ ᝄ ᝄ ᝄ ᝄ ᝄ ᝄ ᝄ ᝄ ᝄ

Directions: Delete (cross out) any prepositional phrases. Underline the subject once and the verb twice.

1. A wolf stood atop a snowy hill and howled.

2. Several tourists stopped by the seals and watched them.

3. This soup is delicious and fights against colds.

4. They jumped off their bikes and rushed down the riverbank.

5. Kevin's fish floats near the top of the tank and blows bubbles.

6. Before the football game, we ate fish and drank lemonade.

7. Oil in the pan heated rapidly and smoked for a few minutes.

8. She swims on a team and competes throughout the state.

9. Their parents are in the flooring business and sell marble tile.

10. He tossed the newspaper onto a front porch and drove to the next house.

11. Our horse lies on its side inside the barn or stands in the meadow.

12. The main speaker smiled and shook my hand during the reception.

12

An **imperative sentence** gives a command.

Continue to cross out prepositional phrases so that you can find the subject and verb.

Example: Take this to the dry cleaner.

Although the word, you, is not stated, it's understood that someone wants **YOU** to do something. It could have been expressed in this manner:

Example: You take this to the dry cleaner.

However, that isn't the way we talk. We usually omit the word, *YOU*.
To show this in written form, we write *you* at the beginning of the sentence, underline it, and place parentheses around it. **(You)**

Example: **(You)** Take this to the dry cleaner.

చిలుకచిలుకచిలుకచిలుకచిలుకచిలుకచిలుకచిలుకచిలుకచిలుకచిలుకచిలుకచిలుక

Directions: Delete (cross out) any prepositional phrases. Underline the subject once and the verb or verb phrase twice.

Remember: verb phrase = helping verb(s) + main verb

(You) 1. Color inside the lines.

(You) 2. Sit with me during lunch.

(You) 3. Drop this coin into that box.

(You) 4. Put this box underneath the table.

(You) 5. Look out the window.

(You) 6. Add two eggs and beat for two minutes.

(You) 7. Do not go without us.

As you have already learned:

To + a noun   =   prepositional phrase   Let's race **to that tree**.
To + a pronoun   =   prepositional phrase   Will you go **with us**?

To + verb is called an **infinitive**. We do not delete an infinitive. We simply place parentheses **(   )** around it.

Examples of infinitives: to add   Micah likes **(to add)**.
                           to pitch   Joanie wants **(to pitch)** first.
                           to think   We have decided **(to think)** about
                                       our project.

&&&&&&&&&&&&&&&&&&&&&&&&&&&&

Directions: Delete (cross out) any prepositional phrases. Underline the subject once and the verb or verb phrase twice. Place any infinitive in parentheses (   ).

1. Those children want (to see) alpacas.

2. Her wish was (to go) to Africa.

3. Jeb's grandparents like (to snowboard.)

4. His goal is (to move) near Miami.

5. Your store needs (to be) in this spot.

6. Several students decided (to rush) through the test.

7. The nurse needs (to take) information from his patient.

8. One teller chose (to stay) at the bank for lunch.

9. You don't have (to run)

10. Tara and Mike might want (to change) their website.

11. Loni wants (to make) flower arrangements with her brother.

14

Name _Amanda Trumble_

Date _Jan 3 2013_   F

Sometimes, a word that usually serves as a preposition will stand alone. This word frequently ends a sentence. Such words as *in, on, off, inside, out, outside, over, through, near, around, by, up,* and *down* can serve as either a preposition (when it begins a phrase) or as an adverb (when it stands alone).

> Examples: We looked **up**.
>
> Come **in**.
>
> Jump **on**.

When a word that usually is a preposition stands alone, it serves as an adverb telling *where*.

> Examples: We looked **up**.   <u>Where</u> did we look?   ***UP!***
>
> Come **in**.   <u>Where</u> are we to come?   ***IN!***
>
> Jump **on**.   <u>Where</u> are we to jump?   ***ON!***

Directions: Write a word that you learned on your list of prepositions in each blank. Label it **Adv.** to show that it serves as an adverb. Then, rewrite the word in the next blank and read that sentence.

1. ~~Hang~~ _Shoot_ _down Adv._   _down_ tells where to ~~hang~~ _shoot_.

2. They went _Through adv_.   _Through_, tells where they went.

3. Stand _by adv_.   _By_ tells where to stand.

4. The dog ran _Over Adv._   _Over_ tells where the dog ran.

5. You may come _around Adv._   _around_ tells where you may come.

6. I jumped _off_.   _Off_ tells where I jumped.

7. His cat sleeps _Outside_.   _outside_ tells where his cat sleeps.

15

Do you remember what a **phrase** is? It's made up of more than one word. A **prepositional phrase** begins with a preposition and ends with a noun (or pronoun). It has to have more than one word.

                                         prepositional phrase

Example: She parks her car *outside her bedroom window*.

When a word that usually is a preposition stands alone, it cannot be part of a prepositional phrase. That word serves as an **adverb** (Adv.).

                                       Adv.

Example: The children rushed outside.

                   Where *did the children rush?* **OUTSIDE!**

Sometimes, a sentence will contain an adverb and no prepositional phrase.

                                       Adv.

Example: We walked **outside** (to talk).

ಶಾಶಾಶಾಶಾಶಾಶಾಶಾ

Sometimes, a sentence will have an adverb and a prepositional phrase side by side. If you see two words that we learned as prepositions next to each other, both (usually) cannot serve as prepositions. One has to be an adverb.

                                    Adv.

Example: She walked **over** ~~to our table~~ and shook my hand.

ಶಾಶಾಶಾಶಾಶಾಶಾಶಾಶಾಶಾಶಾಶಾಶಾಶಾಶಾ

Directions: Delete (cross out) any prepositional phrases. Underline the subject once and the verb twice. Label any adverb that tells *where* – **Adv.**

1. Carl <u>looked</u> up. [Adv.]

2. <u>Mom</u> <u><u>walked</u></u> over ~~to her neighbor's apartment~~. [Adv.]

3. The <u>mechanic</u> <u><u>stooped</u></u> down ~~by the car~~. [Adv.]

4. <u>Hannah</u> <u><u>stayed</u></u> inside ~~during the rain shower~~. [adv]

5. The ~~model~~ [Pilot] <u><u>stepped</u></u> out ~~onto the runway~~. [Adv]

6. A <u>bunny</u> <u><u>snuggled</u></u> in ~~among some soft green bushes~~. [Adv]

7. <u><u>Come</u></u> by ~~for two hours~~. [Adv.]

16

Name _Amanda Trumble_   **Preposition Review**

Date _Feb. 2, 2012_   _S_

A. List of Prepositions:

Directions: Write the prepositions by adding missing letters.

A's

1. About   18. Beyond   **N's**   44. To

2. Above   19. But (meaning   31. Near   45. Toward
                            except)
3. Across   20. By   **O's**   **U's**

4. After   **C's**   32. of   46. Under

5. Against   21. concerning   33. Off   47. underneath

6. Along   **D's**   34. on   48. until

7. Amid   22. Down   35. onto   49. Up

8. Among   23. During   36. out   50. upon

9. Around   **E's**   37. outside

10. At   24. except   38. over   **W's**

11. Atop   **F's**   **P's**   51. with

B's   25. For   39. Past   52. within

12. Before   26. From   **R's**   53. Without

13. Behind   **I's**   40. Regarding

14. Below   27. In   **S's**

15. Beneath   28. Inside   41. since

16. Beside   29. Into   **T's**

17. Between   **L's**   42. Through

                        30. Like   43. Throughout

17

B. **Subject/Verb:**

Directions: Cross out any prepositional phrases. Underline the subject once and the verb twice.

1. Rats ate the corn in the barn.

2. A navy pilot nodded toward the officer.

3. His tennis shoes were under his backpack.

4. Are dogs like a shepherd in great demand?

5. During the meeting, a woman from Kentucky spoke about pollution.

C. **Verb Phrases:**

Directions: Cross out any prepositional phrases. Underline the subject once and the verb phrase twice.

1. She must have caught a fish before noon.

2. Their family is boating at a nearby lake.

3. Joy may want that hose near her car.

You 4. Did the parade come past your house?

D. **Compound Objects of the Preposition:**

Directions: Cross out any prepositional phrases. Underline the subject once and the verb twice.

1. Your shirt with stars and stripes is colorful.

2. A package for my mother and dad arrived.

3. They eat snacks during the morning or the afternoon.

4. Eric played tennis against Rafe and me.

5. A visiting nurse sat between the patient and her son.

18

E. **Compound Subjects:**

Directions: Cross out any prepositional phrases. Underline the subject once and the verb twice.

1. Lanny and Nell live behind them.

2. A man and his friend walked beyond the old cemetery.

3. Her alarm clock and calendar are beside her bed.

4. During their garage sale, Carla and her friends talked about vacations.

5. Several cards and envelopes were under unopened letters.

F. **Compound Verbs:**

Directions: Cross out any prepositional phrases. Underline the subject once and the verb twice.

1. He coughed and blew his nose.

2. A whale eats and swims at the same time.

3. Jessi jumped on the diving board and fell toward the ladder.

4. She stopped by a creek and waded in the water.

5. Rachel stands and waits 10 minutes for the bus every morning.

G. **Imperative Sentences:**

Directions: Cross out any prepositional phrases. Underline the subject once and the verb twice.

1. *you* Keep this in your notebook.

2. *you* Walk to the right of the ladder.

3. *you* Step over the puddle.

4. *you* Wait outside the gym until the end of basketball practice.

19

H. **Infinitives:**

Directions: Cross out any prepositional phrases. Place parentheses around any infinitive. Underline the subject once and the verb twice.

1. They stood (to watch) ~~the soccer game.~~

2. One artist began (to paint) ~~a motorcycle.~~

3. Everyone ~~except Trina~~ likes (to lift) weights.

4. ~~Before breakfast,~~ she sits (to exercise.)

I. **Preposition or Adverb?:**

Directions: Cross out any prepositional phrases. Underline the subject once and the verb twice. Write **A** if the boldfaced word serves as an adverb. Write **P** if the boldfaced word serves as a preposition that begins a prepositional phrase.

1. ___A___   He fell **down**.

2. ___P___   He fell **down** the cellar steps.

3. ___A___   Tara looked **up**.

4. ___P___   Tara looked **up** from her reading.

J. **Verb Phrases and *Not*:**

Directions: Cross out any prepositional phrases. Box *not* or *n't*. Underline the subject once and the verb twice.

1. We could [not] row ~~across the lake~~ ~~after the storm.~~

2. Lynn has[n't] seen Tom ~~since Monday.~~

3. Flowers will [not] be planted ~~along this sidewalk.~~

4. Should[n't] you stand ~~against that wall~~ ~~for this game?~~

20

K. General Review:

Directions: Cross out any prepositional phrases. Underline the subject once and the verb or verb phrase twice.

Example: <u>Do</u> <u>you</u> <u>want</u> (to step) out ~~onto the patio~~?

1. A <u>booklet</u> regarding biking <u>is</u> ~~on your bed~~.

2. <u>I</u> <u>keep</u> bleach ~~on a shelf~~ ~~above my washing machine~~.

3. <u>Everyone</u> ~~but my father~~ slept ~~inside our tent~~.

4. <u>Tami</u> and <u>Dirk</u> <u>will</u> not <u>drive</u> ~~through a wild-animal park~~.

5. <u>Stay</u> ~~within the lines~~ (to color.)

6. <u>We</u> <u>rushed</u> ~~out the door~~ (to the) ice-cream truck.

7. ~~During the party~~, one <u>child</u> <u>danced</u> ~~atop a bench~~.

8. A <u>visitor</u> and her <u>friends</u> <u>walked</u> ~~around the hotel~~ ~~before dinner~~.

9. A ski <u>boat</u> <u>was</u> <u>placed</u> ~~upon a trailer~~ and <u>hauled</u> ~~to a lake~~.

10. The <u>groomer</u> <u>asked</u> questions ~~concerning the dog's health~~.

11. The <u>actor</u> <u>walked</u> ~~onto the stage~~ ~~with the director~~.

12. ~~After the show~~, the <u>singer</u> <u>stood</u> ~~amid several fans~~ and <u>signed</u> autographs.

13. <u>Has</u> <u>Mike</u> <u>placed</u> his tennis racket ~~beneath your chair~~?

14. ~~From my seat~~ ~~near a large window~~, <u>I</u> <u>could</u> not <u>see</u> the speaker.

15. Each <u>student</u> ~~between the ages of six and nine~~ <u>may</u> <u>enter</u> the contest.

16. (You) <u>Don't</u> <u>wait</u> ~~until nighttime~~ (to leave.)

Good writing needs **details**. Prepositional phrases can be used as a tool to provide these.

Sometimes, the details will be near the end of a sentence.

A little boy walked **with his mother**.
          through the woods.
          to his friend's house.

Sometimes, the details will be used near the subject of the sentence.

A little boy **in a blue sailor hat** waved to me.
          from Italy
          under a table

Directions: Write a prepositional phrase to add detail to each sentence. Do not use the same preposition more than once.

1. Patty sat _accros the hated shotriff_ .

2. A man stood _near the house in question_ .

3. That lady _with the black dog,_ is my neighbor.

4. We looked _amied the flowers_ .

5. My father likes to sing _among his friends_ .

6. The cabin _atop that hill_ is new.

7. A large truck sped _over the new brige_ .

8. Those flowers _on Klink's desk._ are pretty.

9. Place the newspaper _in the fire_ .

10. A teacher _from Minnesota_ spoke to us.

22

Good writing uses **vivid details**. The reader should be able to picture descriptions.

Sometimes, we add describing words within a prepositional phrase. These provide vivid details.

> His keys are lying **on a table**.

> His keys are lying **on a <u>long</u>, <u>glass</u> table.**

Notice how details can change a sentence.

> The woman **in an elegant, sequined dress** laughed.

> The woman **in a dirty, frayed dress** laughed.

ৡৡৡৡৡৡৡৡৡৡৡৡৡৡৡৡৡৡৡ

Directions: Rewrite each sentence, adding vivid details within each prepositional phrase. Make each sentence very different.

1. They walked into a house.

   A. _The family walked into the big, brik house for sale._

   B. _They walked cautiously into a old, red barn._

2. Two girls sat near a stream and talked.

   A. _Two small girls sat talking Near a wide, mill stream._

   B. _Two girls sat Near a running, bubbleing, stream talking_

3. A bunny hopped through the weeds.

   A. _A brown bunny hopped through the tall, thin weeds._

   B. _The pet bunny hopped through the huge, green weeds._

To be is an infinitive.   Infinitive = to + verb

A. **When using present time (today):**

With the subject *I*, use *am*.
I **am** funny.

Singular means one. With most singular subjects, use *is*.
Parker **is** funny.   She **is** funny.   It **is** funny.

With the subject *you*, use *are*.
You **are** funny.

Plural means more than one. With a plural subject, use *are*.
Some jokes **are** funny.

B. **When using past time (yesterday):**

With a singular subject, use *was*.
I **was** funny.   Parker **was** funny.   She **was** funny.   It **was** funny.

With *you*, use *were*.
You **were** funny.

With a plural (more than one) subject, use *were*.
Her jokes **were** funny.

৵৵৵৵৵৵৵৵৵৵৵৵৵৵৵৵৵৵৵৵৵৵৵৵

Directions: Write *is, am, are, was,* or *were* in the space provided.

1. Today, Char _____*is*_____ my best friend.

2. Last year, Mrs. Small _____*was*_____ my teacher.

3. The ripe berries _____*are*_____ on that bush.

4. I _____*am*_____ hungry now.

5. Yesterday, many horses _____*were*_____ in the corral.

6. At present, you _____*are*_____ the winner.

7. My parents _____*were*_____ in Santa Fe several years ago.

8. _____*Were*_____ you there last week?

24

The verb of a sentence expresses an action or makes a statement.
Verbs that simply state a fact are often called state-of-being verbs.

    Examples: His mother **bought** several books.   (action)
                    Cooked pasta *is* in that pan.   (statement)

The verb, ***to be***, often makes a statement.
The parts of *to be* are <u>is</u>, <u>am</u>, <u>are</u>, <u>was</u>, <u>were</u>, <u>be</u>, <u>being</u>, and <u>been</u>.

    (Today)   I **am** hungry.   (Yesterday)   I **was** hungry.
               He **is** hungry.   You **were** hungry.
               You **are** hungry.   We **were** hungry.
               We **are** hungry.

Directions: In the space provided, write **Yes** if the boldfaced verb shows action.
                 Write **No** if the boldfaced verb does not show action.

1. _Yes_   The child **rolled** the ball to his parents.

2. _No_   Kami's dad **is** a mailman in their town.

3. _no_   Mrs. Luna **fixes** computers for a living.

4. _No_   Two cherries **were** on the dessert.

5. _yes_   After a few minutes, a waitress **brought** our drinks.

6. _Yes_   Her friend **pans** for gold in the mountains.

7. _Yes_   That boy **walks** to football practice on Saturdays.

8. _no_   Grandma **spoke** with her doctor about a problem.

9. _no_   Spicy chicken wings **are** on the grill.

10. _No_   Kirk **practices** his flute every evening.

11. _Yes_   The gardener **scattered** mulch on the soil.

12. _No_   I **am** glad for you.

CONTRACTIONS

In forming a contraction, we draw together two words to make one word. We do this by dropping a letter or letters and inserting an apostrophe (') where the letter or letters have been left out.

A. Make sure that your apostrophe is slightly curved.

B. The apostrophe must be placed exactly where the letter or letters are missing.

C. Write contractions in broken form so that mistakes are avoided.

didn't   Note the space between <u>n</u> and <u>t</u>. In cursive, do not attach the <u>n</u> and <u>t</u>.

CONTRACTION = VERB + WORD		CONTRACTION = WORD + VERB	
aren't	are + not	he's	he + is
can't	cannot	he'd	he + would
couldn't	could + not	here's	here + is
don't	do + not	I'd	I + would
doesn't	does + not	I'll	I + shall (will)
didn't	did + not	I'm	I + am
hasn't	has + not	it's	it + is
haven't	have + not	I've	I + have
hadn't	had + not	she'd	she + would
isn't	is + not	she's	she + is
mightn't	might + not	there's	there + is
mustn't	must + not	they'll	they + will
shouldn't	should + not	they're	they + are
wasn't	was + not	we're	we + are
weren't	were + not	we've	we + have
won't	will + not	what's	what + is
wouldn't	would + not	where's	where + is
		who's	who + is
		you'll	you + will
		you're	you + are

Name Amanda Trumblet

Date Feb 14 2013   w

A **contraction** is a word made when two words are placed together and shortened.

&&&&&&&&&&&&&&&&&&&&&&&&&&&&&&&&&&&

Directions: Write the contraction.

1. cannot - _ca'nt_ R.H.
2. he is - _he's_
3. have not - _haven't_
4. who is - _who's_
5. did not - _did'nt_
6. will not - _won't_
7. we have - _we've_
8. we are - _we're_
9. I have - _I've_
10. what is - _what's_
11. he would - _he'd_
12. does not - _does'nt_
13. she would - _she'd_
14. was not - _was'nt_
15. I shall (will) - _I'll_
16. there is - _there's_
17. would not - _wouldn't_
18. they will - _they'll_

19. they are - _They're_ L.H.
20. where is - _where's_
21. is not - _is'nt_
22 . should not - _should'nt_
23. he will - _he'll_
24. I am - _I'am_
25. you will - _you'll_
26. had not - _had'nt_
27. you are - _you're_
28. were not - _were'nt_
29. are not - _are'nt_
30. she is - _she's_
31. has not - _has'nt_
32. it is - _it's_
33. you would - _you'd_
34. do not - _do'nt_
35. here is - _here's_
36. I would - _I'd_

Name _Amanda Trumble_   **VERBS**

Date _Feb. 15. 2013_   w   **Contractions**

A. Directions: Write four contractions that begin with the pronoun <u>I</u>.

1. _I'd_   2. _I've_   3. _I'll_   4. _I'm_

B. Directions: Write 17 contractions that end with <u>n't</u>.

1. _Wouldn't_   10. _isn't_

2. _Should'nt_   11. _wasn't_

3. _Couldn't_   12. _weren't_

4. _aren't_   13. _doesn't_

5. _have'nt_   14. _can't_

6. _won't_   15. _Mustn't_

7. _has'nt_   16. _might'nt_

8. _did'nt_   17. _had'nt_

9. _do'nt_

C. Directions: Write three contractions that begin with <u>you</u>.

1. _you'd_   2. _you'll_   3. _you're_

D. Directions: Write three contractions that begin with <u>wh</u>.

1. _what's_   2. _where's_   3. _who's_

E. Directions: Write two contractions that begin with <u>we</u>.

1. _we've_   2. _we're_

F. Directions: Write the following contractions.

1. he is - _he's_   2. there is - _there's_   3. she is - _she's_

28

Name _Amanda Trumblot_   **VERBS**

Date _Feb. 16-2013_   T   **Contractions**

Directions: Write the contraction for the boldfaced words. Then, write an ending for each sentence.

Example: (**Where is**) _Where's_ _your brother_ ?

1. You (**are not**) _aren't going to the pic-nic?_ .

2. (**He is**) _He's going home instead._ .

3. Mike (**cannot**) _can't read without his Lego!_ .

4. (**I am**) _I am showing him how to read anyday!_ .

5. Next year, (**they will**) _they'll go to Kentucy!_ .

6. I think that (**you are**) _you're the best shot of anyone._

7. Hank (**will not**) _won't wait for a bathroom stop!_ .

8. (**What is**) _What's all the noise about_ ?

9. (**Have not**) _Haven't you been loud enough_ ?

10. That car (**does not**) _doesn't need to be fixed_ .

11. (**Who is**) _Who's stolen newkork's wallet_ ?

12. (**I have**) _I've stolen it back already sir!_ .

13. Are you aware that (**it is**) _it's morning_ ?

14. (**You will**) _You'll want a big breckfast_ .

15. Those ideas (**were not**) _weren't smart enough to fool me!_

16. I (**should not**) _shouldn't have trusted you_ .

17. (**They are**) _They're to esey!_ .

29

Directions: Write the contraction for the boldfaced words. Then, write an ending for each sentence.

1. My neighbor (**could not**) _couldn't come to the door_ .

2. (**There is**) _There is another option if you think about it._

3. The waiter (**did not**) _did'nt bring me the right kind of food._

4. (**I shall**) _I'll complament the & Chef_ .

5. During the holiday, (**they are**) _they're going to the Hoffbrau_ .

6. (**Do not**) _Don't look now, but we have the bomb_ .

7. (**We are**) _We're going to blow the brige_ .

8. (**I would**) _I'd give the the war !_ .

9. (**Has not**) _Hasn't you already done that_ ?

10. She (**was not**) _was'nte ready for me to come home_ .

11. (**We have**) _We've decided to blow it anyway_ .

12. (**Is not**) _Isn't There any Jewals?_ ?

13. The child (**would not**) _wouldn't tell me the name of her father_

14. (**I would**) _I'd take them home right away_ .

15. My friends (**were not**) _weren't there to help me_ .

16. (**Here is**) _Here's sunset, and premena'._ .

17. (**They will**) _They'll help me Insted._ .

18. My uncle (**had not**) _hadn't approved when he found out!_ .

T

You're / Your
It's / Its
They're / Their / There

A. **You're** is a contraction meaning you are. **Your** is a possessive pronoun. It will answer: your (what?). A quick way to check your choice in your writing is to say <u>you are</u> in the sentence.

> Examples: You're my buddy.
> **You are** my buddy.　　　　(correct)
>
> **Your** sister called.
> *Your* what?　*Your* sister!　　　(correct)

Could you use <u>you're sister called</u>? Try it. <u>You are sister called.</u> *Incorrect!*

B. **It's** is a contraction meaning it is. **Its** is a possessive pronoun; it will answer: its (what?).

> Examples: It's too hot.　　　(correct)
> **It is** too hot.
>
> The cat licked **its** kitten.　(correct)
> *Its* what? *Its* kitten!

Could you use <u>it's kitten</u>? Try it. <u>The cat licked it is kitten.</u> *Incorrect!*

C. **They're** is a contraction meaning they are. **Their** is a possessive pronoun; it will answer: their (what?).

> Examples: They're ready.　　　　　(correct)
> **They are** ready.
>
> **Their** aunt is the owner of this store.
> *Their* what?　*Their* aunt!　　　　(correct)

Could you use <u>they're aunt</u>? Try it. <u>They are aunt is the owner of this store.</u> *Incorrect!*

There is an adverb that usually tells where.

> Example: I am going **there**.　Where?　There!　(correct)

There may begin a sentence.
> Example: **There** are three magazines for you.

Place the subject at the beginning of the sentence: Three magazines are **there** for you. You still use *there*. Do you see that *there* possibly tells *where*?　31

Name *Amanda Trumble*

Date *Feb 20, 2013*   F

Directions: Write the correct word. If the answer is ***its***, ***your***, or ***their***, draw
          an arrow to the word it modifies (tells *what*).

1.   I'd like to play with (you're, your) ____*Your*____ puppy. *helmet*

2.   When (you're, your) ____*You're*____ ready, please push this button.

3.   (It's, Its) ____*It's*____ raining again in the ~~Northwest~~. *Sherwood*

4.   We went (they're, their, there) ____*There*____ during spring break.

5.   The train blew (it's, its) ____*its*____ whistle several times.

6.   (They're, Their, There) ____*Their*____ friends live near a beach.

7.   Do you know if (they're, their, there) ____*They're*____ learning to ride
    horses?

8.   When the bird hurt (it's, its) ____*its*____ wing, ~~Grandpa~~ took care of
    it. *carter*

9.   ~~Van~~ drank orange juice from (it's, its) ____*its*____ container. *Shakti*

10.   I think (you're, your) ____*You're*____ a very good sport.

11.   Her boss and his wife invited her to (they're, their, there) ____*Their*____
    ~~condo~~. *Stalag*

12.   The ~~deli worker~~ said, "(You're, Your) ____*Your*____ sandwich is
    finished." *Chef*

13.   During autumn, (it's, it's) ____*It's*____ fun to hike in the woods.

14.   When (you're, your) ____*you're*____ hungry, (they're, their, there)

    ____*There*____ are snacks in the pantry.

15.   "(They're, Their, There) ____*There*____ must be a mistake!" ~~she~~
    exclaimed. *He*

32

Name _Amanda Trumble_

Date _Feb. 2/ 2013_   F

A. Directions: Write **it's** or **its** in the blank. If the answer is *its*, draw an arrow to the word it modifies (goes over to that word).

1. _____It's_____ a good idea to wear a jacket today.

2. "At the beginning of every day, _____it's_____ wise to write your goals," the speaker said.

3. The car rolled down the street without _____its_____ driver.

4. The toy was lying on the floor, and _____its_____ front wheels were missing.

5. When I cut a rose, _____its_____ leaves wilted.

B. Directions: Write **you're** or **your** in the blank. If the answer is *your*, draw an arrow to the word it modifies (goes over to that word).

1. Have you been told if _____you're_____ a winner?

2. I wonder if _____your_____ cousin joined the U. S. Army.

3. "_____You're_____ not hurt," said the mother to the child.

4. _____Your_____ friend hasn't ridden a subway yet.

C. Directions: Write **they're, their,** or **there** in the blank. If the answer is *their*, draw an arrow to the word it modifies (goes over to that word).

1. I believe that _____They're_____ from Newberg, Oregon.

2. _____Their_____ neighbor owns a boat _____There_____.

3. _____There_____ have been no earthquakes in southern England.

4. Are you sure that _____They're_____ visiting Key West?

5. Did a clerk ask for _____Their_____ money?

AUXILIARY (HELPING) VERBS

You will need to learn these auxiliary (helping) verbs:

do	has	may	can	could	is	were
does	have	might	shall	should	am	be
did	had	must	will	would	are	being
					was	been

VERB PHRASE

A verb phrase is composed of one or more helping verbs plus a main verb.

The **main verb** is the last part of a verb phrase.

Examples: They <u>were</u> **talking** loudly.

The <u>doctor</u> <u>must have</u> **left** ~~for the day~~.

verb phrase	**=**	**helping verb(s)**	**+**	**main verb**
were talking	=	were		talking
must have left	=	must have		left

A.   Continue to cross out prepositional phrases. They won't be part of a verb phrase.

B.   Sometimes, a verb that can be a helping verb will stand alone in a sentence.

<u>Are</u> those hamster yours?   In this sentence, <u>are</u> is the only verb. There is no verb phrase. *Are* is the main verb.

<u>Are</u> we <u>staying</u> ~~until noon~~?   In this sentence, *are* is a helping verb; <u>are staying</u> is the verb phrase.

C.   If the sentence is interrogative (asks a question), look for a helping verb **at or near the beginning** of the sentence. It may be helpful to restate the sentence in declarative (statement) form in order to determine the verb phrase more easily.

Example: <u>Have</u> you <u>signed</u> your name?   You <u>have signed</u> your name.

D.   **<u>Not</u>** or **<u>n't</u>** is never part of a verb phrase. *Not* is an adverb. **Box <u>not</u> or <u>n't</u>**. Do not underline it as part of a verb phrase.

Example: The game <u>did</u> **| not |** <u>begin</u> ~~on time~~.

E.   Sometimes, a word might look like it should be part of a verb phrase.

Example: This apple <u>is bad</u>.   (incorrect)
This apple <u>is</u> bad.   (correct)

To test if a word can possibly be a verb, place *to* in front of the main verb: (to bad). Then, conjugate the verb by saying: "To bad: Today, I bad.
Yesterday, I badded.
Tomorrow, I shall bad."

To bad can't be conjugated; *bad* is not part of the verb phrase.   35

Name _Amanda Tremblay_

Date _Feb. 25. 2013_   _5_

A verb phrase is made up of one or more helping verbs plus a main verb. The **main verb** is the last part of a verb phrase.

A. Directions: A helping verb appears in boldfaced print. Write an appropriate main verb and underline the verb phrase twice.

1. The vacuum cleaner **was** _left_ in the hallway.

2. Several children **had** _looked_ at me.

3. She **may** _turn_ in an hour.

4. You **should** _work_ every day.

5. The baby **did** not _cry_ for three hours.

6. **Does** Madison _go_ our school?

7. I **might** _run_ today.

B. Directions: Write an appropriate main verb and underline the verb phrase twice.

1. I should have _waited_ .

2. Were you _on time_ ?

3. The karate expert is _to go_ next.

4. Your short story might be _long_ .

5. His brothers don't _look_ well.

6. Deka may have been _talking_ with her aunt.

7. That bush has not _been seen_ recently.

8. The bus must have _arrived_ early.

36

A verb phrase is made up of one or more helping verbs plus a main verb. The **main verb** is the last part of a verb phrase.

Directions: Cross out any prepositional phrases. Underline the subject once and the verb phrase twice. Be sure to box *not* or *n't*.

Example: We might be going to the beach tomorrow.

1. A police officer may have stopped a speeder.

2. Two workers were welding two metal pieces.

3. Jane's father has won a cooking award.

4. Do you eat lunch at a mall?

5. Her shirt had slipped from the ironing board.

6. This computer is not working.

7. Does Toby live beside a church?

8. One designer has been working on a folding sofa.

9. Would you ever use a screwdriver without a handle?

10. A bulldozer can move that mound of dirt.

11. Plastic will be wrapped around a box.

12. I should not have told anyone about my idea.

13. Wasn't Mary practicing for the relay today?

14. Fireworks are being planned for the Fourth of July.

15. Shall I find my guitar for you?

16. Loni might have gone with her grandfather.

37

Directions: Cross out any prepositional phrases. Underline the subject once and the verb phrase twice. Be sure to box *not* or *n't*.

Example: One of the birds is perched on their brick wall.

1. I am reading booklets about Canada

2. Pressure must be placed on the bleeding arm. (Leg)

3. May I order an English muffin without butter?

4. Lance (Tuck) could not have walked there in five minutes.

5. Several walnut trees (bands) have been planted near a stream within the city park.

6. Did Erin move from Santa Fe to Long Beach?

7. Dad (Sharlet) has shopped at two stores for our groceries.

8. Her father-in-law is driving a van without a rear-view mirror.

9. Marsha (Hilda) should have dropped these cards into a nearby mailbox.

10. Are you frying or broiling the fish?

11. Lucy (Auntie) must have knitted Kim (Hogan) a scarf (socks) for a birthday present.

12. Weren't your puppies born on New Year's Eve?

13. A cow and its calf must have been taken to another meadow.

14. A security guard would have checked all stores in the mall.

15. Double-decker buses (lincoln green) (outback) are running through London's streets.

16. That guitar has been signed by a famous musician. (Alert-a-date)

17. (you) Call me after your soccer game.

38

Name _Amanda Trumblet_

Date _Nov. 19, 2013_

Regular and Irregular Verbs

A regular verb adds <u>ed</u> to the past tense. You have learned that tense means time. Past tense refers to something that has already happened.

Examples: to laugh   Mona laugh**ed** for several minutes.
           to stir   Mona stirr**ed** pancake batter.

Important: Some regular verbs end in <u>e</u>. To form the past tense, drop the final <u>e</u> and add **ed**.

Examples: to lik<u>e</u> - lik**ed**
           to escap<u>e</u> - escap**ed**

An irregular verb does not add <u>ed</u> to the past tense. In fact, it usually changes form for both the past tense and part of a verb called the past participle. (Past participle is the form made by placing words like *has*, *have*, or *had* in front of a verb.)

Examples: to know   Bo know**ed** the answer.   (Incorrect)
                        Bo **knew** the answer.   (Correct)

                        Bo has know**ed** her for a long time.   (Incorrect)
                        Bo has **known** her for a long time.   (Correct)

Directions: Write the past tense (time) in the blank. Then, write **R** if the verb is regular and **I** if the verb is irregular.

Example: to smile - ___**smiled**___   ___**R**___

1. to pull - _pulled_   _R_
2. to give - _given_   _I_
3. to ring - _rang_   _I_
4. to believe - _believed_   _R_
5. to break - _broke_   _I_
6. to write - _wrote_   _I_
7. to search - _searched_   _R_
8. to lock - _locked_   _R_
9. to hit - _hit_   _I_
10. to find - _found_   _R_
11. to erase - _erased_   _R_
12. to cut - _cuted_   _I_
13. to tap - _Taped_   _R_
14. to tape - _taped_   _R_

39

Name *Amanda Trumble* ✱

Date *Nov. 19, 2013*   *m*

Pre/Post Quiz - Irregular Verbs

A present participle is formed by adding <u>ing</u> *to a verb (example: to go =* <u>going</u>*). The past participle is formed by placing* <u>had</u> *in front of a verb (had* <u>gone</u>*).*

Directions: Write the past participle form for each verb.

(en)

Infinitive	Present	Past	Present Participle	Past Participle*
To be	is, am, are	was, were	being	1. (had) been
To beat	beat(s)	beat	beating	2. (had) beatten
To begin	begin(s)	began	beginning	3. (had) begune
To blow	blow(s)	blew	blowing	4. (had) blown
To break	break(s)	broke	breaking	5. (had) broken
To bring	bring(s)	brought	bringing	6. (had) brought
To burst	burst(s)	burst	bursting	7. (had) burst
To buy	buy(s)	bought	buying	8. (had) bought
To choose	choose(s)	chose	choosing	9. (had) choose
To come	come(s)	came	coming	10. (had) came
To do	do, does	did	doing	11. (had) did
To drink	drink(s)	drank	drinking	12. (had) drank
To drive	drive(s)	drove	driving	13. (had) drove
To eat	eat(s)	ate	eating	14. (had) ate
To fall	fall(s)	fell	falling	15. (had) fell
To find	find(s)	found	finding	16. (had) found
To fly	fly, flies	flew	flying	17. (had) flew
To freeze	freeze(s)	froze	freezing	18. (had) frozen
To give	give(s)	gave	giving	19. (had) givin
To go	go, goes	went	going	20. (had) gone
To grow	grow(s)	grew	growing	21. (had) grown
To have	have, has	had	having	22. (had) had
To hang	hang(s)	hung**	hanging	23. (had) hung

Uses a helping verb such as *has*, *have*, or *had*.
**Use the form of *to hang* when it means *to place an object*.

40

Nov. 20. 2013

Infinitive	Present	Past	Present Participle	Past Participle*
To know	know(s)	knew	knowing	24. (had) known
To lay	lay(s)	laid	laying	25. (had) laid
To leave	leave(s)	left	leaving – a house guest	26. (had) left
To lie**	lie(s)	lay	lying	27. (had) lay
To ride	ride(s)	rode	riding	28. (had) ridden
To ring	ring(s)	rang	ringing	29. (had) rung
To rise	rise(s)	rose	rising	30. (had) risen
To run	run(s)	ran	running	31. (had) ran
To see	see(s)	saw	seeing	32. (had) seen
To set	set(s)	set	setting – movie crew	33. (had) set
To shake	shake(s)	shook	shaking	34. (had) shaken
To sing	sing(s)	sang	singing	35. (had) sung
To sink	sink(s)	sank – Titanic	sinking	36. (had) sunken
To sit	sit(s)	sat	sitting	37. (had) sat
To speak	speak(s)	spoke	speaking	38. (had) spoken
To spring	spring(s)	sprang	springing – Actors	39. (had) sprung
To steal	steal(s)	stole	stealing	40. (had) stolen
To swim	swim(s)	swam	swimming	41. (had) swum
To swear	swear(s)	swore	swearing	42. (had) sworn
To take	take(s)	took	taking	43. (had) taken
To teach	teach(es)	taught	teaching	44. (had) taught
To throw	throw(s)	threw	throwing	45. (had) thrown
To wear	wear(s)	wore	wearing – used clothes	46. (had) worn
To write	write(s)	wrote	writing	47. (had) written

*Uses a helping verb such as *has, have,* or *had*.
**meaning *to rest*

41

IRREGULAR VERBS

Infinitive	Present	Past	Present Participle	Past Participle*
To be	is, am, are	was, were	being	been
To beat	beat(s)	beat	beating	beaten
To begin	begin(s)	began	beginning	begun
To blow	blow(s)	blew	blowing	blown
To break	break(s)	broke	breaking	broken
To bring	bring(s)	brought	bringing	brought
To burst	burst(s)	burst	bursting	burst
To buy	buy(s)	bought	buying	bought
To choose	choose(s)	chose	choosing	chosen
To come	come(s)	came	coming	come
To do	do, does	did	doing	done
To drink	drink(s)	drank	drinking	drunk
To drive	drive(s)	drove	driving	driven
To eat	eat(s)	ate	eating	eaten
To fall	fall(s)	fell	falling	fallen
To find	find(s)	found	finding	found
To fly	fly, flies	flew	flying	flown
To freeze	freeze(s)	froze	freezing	frozen
To give	give(s)	gave	giving	given
To go	go, goes	went	going	gone
To grow	grow(s)	grew	growing	grown
To have	have, has	had	having	had
To hang	hang(s)	hung**	hanging	hung**

*Uses a helping verb such as *has*, *have*, or *had*.

A present participle is formed by adding ing *to a verb (example: to go =* going*). The past participle is formed by placing* had *in front of a verb (had* gone*).*

**Use *hung* when referring to objects.

IRREGULAR VERBS

Infinitive	Present	Past	Present Participle	Past Participle*
To know	know(s)	knew	knowing	known
To lay	lay(s)	laid	laying	laid
To leave	leave(s)	left	leaving	left
To lie**	lie(s)	lay	lying	lain
To ride	ride(s)	rode	riding	ridden
To ring	ring(s)	rang	ringing	rung
To rise	rise(s)	rose	rising	risen
To run	run(s)	ran	running	run
To see	see(s)	saw	seeing	seen
To set	set(s)	set	setting	set
To shake	shake(s)	shook	shaking	shaken
To sing	sing(s)	sang	singing	sung
To sink	sink(s)	sank	sinking	sunk
To sit	sit(s)	sat	sitting	sat
To speak	speak(s)	spoke	speaking	spoken
To spring	spring(s)	sprang	springing	sprung
To steal	steal(s)	stole	stealing	stolen
To swim	swim(s)	swam	swimming	swum
To swear	swear(s)	swore	swearing	sworn
To take	take(s)	took	taking	taken
To teach	teach(es)	taught	teaching	taught
To throw	throw(s)	threw	throwing	thrown
To wear	wear(s)	wore	wearing	worn
To write	write(s)	wrote	writing	written

*Uses a helping verb such as *has*, *have*, or *had*. (The tense that *to have* + *the past participle* forms is called the *perfect tense*. You will not learn the *perfect tense* this year.)

**meaning to rest

Note: There are other irregular verbs. Consult a dictionary if you are unsure.

Name Amanda Trumble

Date February 26 2014

Directions: Write the appropriate past participle. Then, underline the
verb phrase twice.

1.   (to choose)   The homeowner had __chosen__ wood flooring.

2.   (to ride)   Nan and Van had __ridin__ all morning.

3.   (to leave)   Marco would have __left__ a note.

4.   (to eat)   Tugs must have __eaten__ all his dog food.

5.   (to wear)   Her back tire was __worn__ down.

6.   (to go)   They could have __gone__ with their uncle.

7.   (to begin)   Many swimmers had __begun__ to shiver.

8.   (to come)   Their guest might have __come__ late.

9.   (to speak)   Cross words must have been __spoken__.

10.   (to drive)   You should have __drivin__ faster.

11.   (to see)   Has he ever __seen__ a dragonfly?

12.   (to fly)   I could not have __flown__ on another flight.

13.   (to drink)   The infant might have __drank__ her formula.

14.   (to rise)   All of the bicycle racers had __risin__ by
six o'clock.

15.   (to throw)   Would your sister have __thrown__ that?

16.   (to fall)   By next week, all of the leaves will have __fallen__.

17.   (to find)   A hiker may have __found__ a piece of old
pottery.

Directions: Cross out any prepositional phrases. Underline the subject
once and the verb phrase twice.

Example: The church <u>bells</u> <u>have</u> already (rang, <u>rung</u>).

1.   The <u>balloon</u> <u>had</u> (busted, burst) ~~from the heat~~.

2.   <u>Have</u> <u>you</u> (did, done) your homework?

3.   <u>Juice</u> <u>has been</u> (frozen, froze) into popsicles.

4.   <u>I</u> <u>should have</u> (ran, run) ~~in the last race~~.

5.   His <u>wallet</u> <u>had been</u> (stolen, stole) yesterday.

6.   This <u>lamp</u> <u>may have been</u> (brung, brought) ~~to America by their grandmother~~.

7.   <u>Can</u> those <u>flowers</u> <u>be</u> (grown, grew) ~~in such a small pot~~?

8.   The <u>milkshakes</u> <u>had been</u> (shook, shaken) ~~in a blender~~.

9.   <u>He</u> <u>must have</u> (written, wrote) ~~for a free booklet~~.

10.   Several <u>songs</u> <u>were</u> (sang, sung) ~~before the program~~.

11.   <u>Could</u> <u>Mr. Frim</u> <u>have</u> (taken, took) the wrong train?

12.   <u>Has</u> your <u>family</u> ever (swam, swum) ~~in Bear Lake~~?

13.   This <u>package</u> <u>might have</u> (come, came) ~~without a zip code~~.

14.   <u>He</u> <u>would</u> not <u>have</u> (known, knew) ~~about this accident~~.

15.   Their <u>taxi</u> <u>had</u> (broke, broken) ~~down along a small canal~~.

16.   ~~By tomorrow~~, <u>she</u> <u>will have</u> (gave, given) her speech three times.

A. Directions: Write a direct object for each sentence. Cross out any prepositional phrases. Underline the subject once and the verb twice. Label the direct object – **D.O.**

1. A cook made a ___ _haggis_ ___.
   D.O.

2. I dropped my ___ _milk_ ___ on the tile floor.
   D.O.

3. She loves her ___ _pigions_ ___ with all her heart.
   D.O.

4. Jenny eats ___ _soup_ ___ for breakfast.
   D.O.

5. One gardener picked ___ _turnips_ ___ in her garden.
   D.O.

B. Directions: Cross out any prepositional phrases. Underline the subject once and the verb or verb phrase twice. Label the direct object – **D.O.**

1. Several scuba divers checked their gear.
   D.O.

2. The toddlers hugged their puppy.
   D.O.

3. The camper placed logs by the fire.

4. We are sanding a rusted chair.
   D.O.

5. The decorator hung baskets on the patio wall.
   D.O.

6. One hotel guest used a private elevator.
   D.O.

7. Usually, the family lights candles during the evening.
   D.O.

8. The post office manager placed a stamp on an envelope.
   D.O.

Victor 9. Jody is carving a wooden bowl. *D.O*

10. A golfer carried her clubs to a golf cart.
    D.O.

11. Three workers washed windows high above the street.
    D.O.

46

Directions: Cross out any prepositional phrases. Underline the subject once and the verb or verb phrase twice. Label the direct object – **D.O.**

                                                D.O.
Example: Hannah leaned her bat ~~against a tree~~.

1. Mark set his car alarm. *(D.O.)*

2. Brittany played a game ~~on the computer~~. ~~Table~~ *(D.O.)*

3. An actor wrote a novel ~~about Hollywood~~. his father *(D.O)*

4. The mother laid the baby ~~in a cradle~~. *(D.O.)*

5. Our dog chased a butterfly ~~across our lawn~~. *(D.O.)*

6. The car dealer hid the keys ~~under the seat~~. *(D.O.)*

7. ~~Mary~~ Marian grooms her horse ~~with great care~~. *(D.O.)*

8. You do not need a partner ~~for this activity~~. *(D.O.)*

9. They started the softball game ~~without me~~. *(Shell / D.O.)*

10. Hasn't Charlie found a summer job? *(D.O.)*

11. Mrs. Landis published an article regarding healthy food. *(D.O.)*

12. Their puppy must have chewed a hole ~~near the corner of the sofa~~. *(D.O.)*

13. Annie and Juan should not have taken a vacation to Phoenix ~~in the summer~~. *(D.O.)*

14. ~~After a long lunch~~, the storeowner lifted bolts ~~of fabric onto racks~~. *(D.O.)*

15. (You) Place this sign ~~across the street and beneath that pine tree~~. *(D.O.)*

Sit/Set
Rise/Raise
Lie/Lay

Sit/Set:

To sit means to rest.

To set means to place or put.

Infinitive	Present	Past	Present Participle	Past Participle
to sit	sit(s)	sat	sitting	(had) sat
to set	set(s)	set	setting	(had) set

Examples: He (sits, sets) near a window.

He (<u>sits</u>, sets) ~~near a window~~.

(There is no direct object. He "rests" near a window.)

To set requires a direct object.

She (sat, set) the timer.
                    D.O.
She (sat, <u>set</u>) the timer.

(When using *set*, label the direct object. What is the object she set?
Answer: timer)

Rise/Raise:

To rise means to go up without help.

To raise means to lift or go up (with help).

Infinitive	Present	Past	Present Participle	Past Participle
to rise	rise(s)	rose	rising	(had) risen ·
to raise	raise(s)	raised	raising	(had) raised

Examples: Smoke (rises, raises) in the air.

Smoke (<u>rises</u>, raises) ~~in the air~~.

Smoke goes up on its own. With *raises*, there must be a direct object. Because *in the air* has been deleted, the sentence can't contain a direct object.

48

To raise requires a direct object.

Mr. Clay (rose, raised) his hand.

D.O.

Mr. Clay (rose, <u>raised</u>) his hand.

With *to raise*, a direct object is required. What did Mr. Clay raise? Answer: hand

Lie/Lay:

To lie means to rest.

To lay means to place.

Infinitive	Present	Past	Present Participle	Past Participle
to lie	lie(s)	lay	lying	(had) lain
to lay	lay(s)	laid	laying	(had) laid

To lie means <u>to rest</u>. Try inserting *rest* or *rests* when you are using *lie* in a sentence.

To lay means <u>to place</u>. **To lay needs a direct object**; there must be an object to place.

Lays, laid, and laying will have a direct object. Lay will have a direct object if it means to place.

Examples:

Ned (lies, lays) tile for a living.

D.O.

Ned (lies, <u>lays</u>) tile ~~for a living~~.

With <u>lays</u>, you must have a direct object.
What is the object Ned places? Answer: tile

Look at *laid* and *lain*:

He had (laid, lain) on a pool float.

He <u>had</u> (laid, <u>lain</u>) ~~on a pool float~~.

Lain refers to resting. (He had *rested* on a pool float.) Also, *on a pool float* has been deleted. Therefore, there is no direct object. To use *laid*, there must be a direct object in the sentence.

VERBS

Sit/Set, Rise/Raise
Lie/Lay

Occasionally, there will be two or more direct objects in a sentence. This is called a compound direct object.

                                          D.O.   D.O.
          Example: Dad <u>spread</u> butter and jam ~~on our toast~~.

A. Directions: Cross out any prepositional phrases. Underline the subject once
                  and the verb twice.   Label any direct object – **D.O.**

1. ~~During the rehearsal dinner~~, the <u>bride</u> <u>kissed</u> her mom and dad ~~on the cheek~~.
                                                        D.O   *D.O.*

2. The <u>twins</u> <u>received</u> flowers and balloons ~~from their grandparents.~~
                              D.O.   *D.O.*

3. <u>Joel</u> <u>grabbed</u> an apple and a granola bar and ran ~~out the door~~.
                       D.O   *D.O*

B. Directions: Cross out any prepositional phrases. Underline the subject once
                  and the verb or verb phrase twice.   Label any direct object – **D.O.**

**Remember: With _to lay_ (_lays, laid, laying_), _to set_, and _to raise_, you must have a direct
              object. If the verb means _to place_, it must have a direct object.**

1. A <u>detective</u> (sat, (set)) ~~several papers by his desk~~.
                                     D.O.

2. Your <u>paintbrush</u> <u>is</u> ((lying,) laying) ~~by your pastel chalks~~.
                                D.O.

3. The <u>conductor</u> (rose, (raised)) his baton.
                                            D.O

4. Their <u>dog</u> (lay, (laid)) his head ~~on my lap~~.
                                   D.O

5. Tara <u>had</u> (laid, (lain)) ~~under her beach umbrella for several hours~~.
                                              D.O.

6. Our <u>friend</u> (rises, (raises)) longhorn cattle and goats.
                                          D.O.   *D.O.*

7. ~~During their morning walk~~, <u>smoke</u> ((rose,) raised) ~~from many chimneys~~.
                                                                        D.O.

8. ((Sit,) Set) ~~along the low wall past the small wooden bridge~~.
                                D.O.

Name *Amanda Tremblet*

Date 3/10/14

VERBS

Sit/Set, Rise/Raise
Lie/Lay

Directions: Cross out any prepositional phrases. Underline the subject once and the verb twice.   Label any direct object – **D.O.**

Remember: **With *to lay* (*lays, laying, laid*), *to set*, and *to raise*, you must have a direct object.**

Example: I am (sitting, setting) your lunch on the counter.

1. A small snake (lay, laid) under a porch swing.

2. Steam (rose, raised) from the kettle.

3. Everyone except Ronny is (sitting, setting) amid that clump of trees.

4. Lucy has been (lying, laying) brick between her patio and shed.

5. Before his marriage, Mr. Lane (raised, rose) sheep in Montana.

6. He (sat, set) across the aisle from me after art class.

7. The baby (lay, laid) his head against his mother's arm.

8. The waiters are (setting, sitting) the tables within a small garden.

9. Have you (laid, lain) on a futon bed?

10. Her voice had (rose, risen) to a high pitch.

11. Justin must have (set, sat) beside his sister during church service.

12. My neighbor's dog (lies, lays) outside her front door after breakfast.

13. One gardener (raises, rises) orchids in his greenhouse.

14. That hotel maid (lies, lays) blankets over the backs of chairs.

15. A mechanic (sat, set) the car parts on a bench by a window.

51

VERB TENSES
Tense means time.

Present Tense:

Present tense means **present time.** Although present can mean at this moment, it is easier to use "today" for present time. Present tense never has a helping verb.

To form the present tense, remove *to* from the infinitive: (infinitive = *to + verb*)

1. **If the subject is singular (one), add <u>s</u> to the verb (<u>es</u> to some).**

    Examples: to make   Their <u>cat</u> <u>makes</u> strange noises. (one animal)
    to turn   He <u>turns</u> left ~~on Potter Street~~.   (one person)

2. **If the subject is <u>you</u>, <u>I</u>, or <u>plural</u> (more than one), simply remove the *to* from the infinitive.**

    Example: to drink   **You** <u>drink</u> water very slowly.
    I <u>drink</u> green tea.
    They <u>drink</u> bottled water.

Past Tense:

Past tense indicates time that **has happened**. Although past can mean a second ago, it is easier to use the term, "yesterday." Past tense never has a helping verb.

1. **To form the past tense of a regular verb, add <u>ed</u> to the verb.**
    If the verb ends in <u>e</u>, drop the final <u>e</u> and add <u>ed</u>.

    to start   A small boy <u>start**ed**</u> to play.
    to change   I <u>chang**ed**</u> a bandage ~~on my foot~~.

2. **To form the past tense of an irregular verb, change the verb to its appropriate form.**

    to teach   Her great uncle <u>taught</u> ~~in a one room school~~.
    to freeze   We <u>froze</u> a circle ~~of ice for the punch~~.

Future Tense:

Future tense indicates **time yet to happen**. There are two helping verbs that indicate future tense: *shall* and *will*. Future may be any time yet to occur; however, to make it easier, we shall use "tomorrow" as a guide.

1. *Will* is most frequently used in forming the future tense.
2. *Shall* is used with the pronoun, *I*. (I <u>shall ask</u> my mother.)
    Shall may be used with *we*.

52

Directions: Write the present, past, and future tense of each verb.

1. **to smell**

   A. *present*   That old <u>cellar</u> _smells_ musty.

   B. *past*   The <u>kitchen</u> _smelled_ like bleach.

   C. *future*   <u>You</u> _shall smell_ fresh after a shower.

2. **to blend**

   A. *present*   This <u>tile</u> _blends well_ with the carpeting.

   B. *past*   <u>Peter</u> _blended_ a protein drink.

   C. *future*   <u>I</u> _will blend_ some herbs for tea.

3. **to scrub**

   A. *present*   <u>Doctors</u> _scrub_ before surgery.

   B. *past*   <u>She</u> _scrubed_ her toes with a loofa.

   C. *future*   A <u>janitor</u> _will scrub_ the mark from the floor.

4. **to do**

   A. *present*   <u>Dave</u> _does_ his dishes every night.

   B. *past*   A <u>friend</u> _did_ the actress's make-up.

   C. *future*   <u>She</u> _will do_ the data sheet tonight.

5. **to laugh**

   A. *present*   <u>Erica</u> _laughs_ frequently.

   B. *past*   <u>Mrs. Lambini</u> _laughed_ softly.

   C. *future*   Your <u>friend</u> _might laugh_ at your excuse.

Present tense means now.

A. Directions: Cross out any prepositional phrases. Underline the subject once. Write the present tense of each verb.

1. Lani (to spend) ___spends her___ summers in Kansas.

2. I (to want) ___want___ a rabbit ~~with floppy ears~~.

3. You (to eat) ___eat___ too fast.

4. Their two spaniels (to greet) ___greet___ us ~~by the front door~~.

🙞🙞🙞🙞🙞🙞🙞🙞🙞🙞🙞🙞🙞🙞🙞🙞🙞🙞

Past tense means past time.

B. Directions: Cross out any prepositional phrases. Underline the subject once. Write the past tense of each verb.

1. The driver (to listen) ___listened___ ~~to the radio~~.

2. Several wild geese (to fly) ___flew___ ~~above our house~~.

3. My cousin (to buy) ___bought___ squash ~~at a farmer's market~~.

4. The host (to reach) ___reached___ ~~across the table~~.

🙞🙞🙞🙞🙞🙞🙞🙞🙞🙞🙞🙞🙞🙞🙞🙞🙞🙞

Future tense means time yet to occur.

C. Directions: Cross out any prepositional phrases. Underline the subject once. Write the future tense of each verb.

1. A doctor (to examine) ___shall examine___ your rash.

2. ~~After dinner~~, I (to send) ___shall send___ you an email.

3. ~~Before college~~, her brother (to work) ___will work___ with my dad.

54

Directions: Cross out any prepositional phrases. Underline the subject once and the verb or verb phrase twice. Write *present*, *past*, or *future* to show the verb tense.

to leave

1. ___*past*___ Joe left ~~in a small blue truck~~.

2. ___*future*___ Everyone ~~but Carlo~~ will leave.

3. ___*present*___ He leaves his jacket ~~inside the front closet~~.

to place

1. ___*Present*___ Mom places our lunches ~~near the door~~.

2. ___*past*___ She placed her drawings ~~beside an art book~~.

3. ___*future*___ ~~For the wedding~~, a florist will place roses ~~throughout the chapel~~.

to punch

1. ___*past*___ The boxer punched the bag hard.

2. ___*future*___ Will you punch holes ~~at the top~~ ~~of this paper~~?

3. ___*present*___ An attendant punches stars ~~in each ticket~~.

to drive

1. ___*future*___ Shannon will drive Mrs. Hill ~~to the airport~~.

2. ___*past*___ The teenager drove ~~through the parking lot~~.

3. ___*present*___ They drive ~~under a narrow freeway bridge~~ ~~during heavy traffic~~.

55

Directions: Write the correct tense.

1. _dumped_   We (past tense of *to dump*) water on our fire.

2. _veers_   This car (present tense of *to veer*) to the left.

3. _dripped_   Suds (past tense of *to drip*) down his finger.

4. _shall record_   Their aunt (future tense of *to record*) a play for their family to watch later.

5. _hauls_   Trena (present tense of *to haul*) wood.

6. _waded_   Birds (past tense of *to wade*) in a lagoon.

7. _whispers_   They (present tense of *to whisper*) loudly.

8. _Shall speak_   I (future of *to speak*) with the officer in charge.

9. _oozed_   Glue (past tense of *to ooze*) from the bottle without a cap.

10. _live_   Six wild parakeets (present tense of *to live*) in that tree.

11. _changes_   Grandma (present tense of *to change*) her oil.

12. _will thank_   You (future tense of *to thank*) us later.

13. _are_   My toes (present tense of *to be*) cold.

14. _went_   Carlotta (past tense of *to go*) to a car show after her track meet.

15. _dissolves_   This gelatin (future tense of *to dissolve*) easily.

16. _grows_   Only one tomato (present tense of *to grow*) in her garden.

You need to learn the conjugation of *to be*: **is, am, are, was, were, be,** **being,** and **_been_**.

Present Tense:

Singular:	**is**	That parking <u>meter</u> <u>is</u> new.
	am	I <u>am</u> a runner.
Plural:	**are**	These <u>pieces</u> of timber <u>are</u> from an old barn.

Past Tense:

Singular:	**was**	My <u>thumb</u> <u>was</u> in a bandage for two days.
Plural:	**were**	Seven <u>secretaries</u> <u>were</u> from an agency.

Future Tense: **be**   I <u>shall be</u> there soon.
                                  The <u>weather</u> <u>will be</u> good tomorrow.

The present participle of *to be* is *being*; the past participle of *to be* is *been*. These are used with a helping verb or verbs to form more complex tenses.

Examples: You <u>are being</u> very silly.
                     I <u>have been</u> to Dover twice.

Been can also be used as an auxiliary (helping) verb:

Example: I <u>must have been doing</u> that wrong.

க்ஷ்க்ஷ்க்ஷ்க்ஷ்க்ஷ்க்ஷ்க்ஷ்க்ஷ்க்ஷ்க்ஷ்க்ஷ்க்ஷ்க்ஷ்க்ஷ்க்ஷ்

Directions: Write the correct form of *to be* in the blank.

1. Yesterday, I _____*was*_____ at an art museum in Seattle.

2. You _____*are*_____ now at the intersection of Bill Road and Bo Street.

3. I _____*am*_____ here now.

4. _____*Will*_____ your team in the playoffs today?

5. Marco and his brother _____*will be*_____ here next month.

6. Last week, all of the writers _____*were*_____ in a meeting.

7. They _____*are*_____ currently in the market for a new home.

Linking Verbs

Action verbs do just as the name states; they show action.

Linking verbs do not show action; they usually make a statement.

Linking Verbs:

to feel	to smell	to grow	to stay
to taste	to seem	to remain	to become
to look	to sound	to appear	to be (is, am, are, was, were, be, being, been)

Some verbs can be used as **either** a linking **verb or** an action verb. If you aren't sure, do this:

A.   First, see if the verb is on the list. If it isn't on the list, do **not** mark it as linking.

Example: Chessa <u>shouted</u> to her friends.

Shouted is not on the linking verb list.

B.   If the verb is on the list, try the technique of replacing it with a form of *to be*. (*Is, am, are, was,* or *were* usually works!) If this can be done *without changing the meaning of the sentence*, the verb is usually linking.

Example: This pear <u>tastes</u> bitter.

To taste is on the list. Now, place a form of *to be* above *tastes*.

is
Example: This pear <u>tastes</u> bitter.

Replacing *tastes* with *is* does not change the meaning of the sentence. Now, look to see if *tastes* links *pear* with *bitter*. We can say ***bitter pear***. *Tastes* is a linking verb here.

58

Try this process with the next sentence:

Example: My dad always <u>tastes</u> his homemade soup.

To taste is on the list. Now, place a form of *to be* above *tastes*.

is

Example: My dad always <u>tastes</u> his homemade soup.

Replacing *tastes* with *is* definitely changes the meaning of the sentence. *Tastes* here shows action; it is **not** a linking verb.

This process should help you to determine if a verb is an action verb or a linking verb.

This is important because **after a linking verb**, you might use an adjective. This adjective will be a describing word.

He is a **slow** runner.   (adjective)
The runner is **slow**.   (adjective)

You add **ly** to *slow* to make it an adverb.

He runs **slowly**.   (adverb telling **how** he runs)

	Adjective	**Adverb**
Examples:	glad	gladly
	happy	happily
	certain	certainly
	legal	legally

Some adverbs that tell how do not add **ly**.

Examples:	fast	He is a **fast** runner.	(adjective)
		He runs **fast**.	(adverb)
	hard	I am a **hard** hitter.	(adjective)
		I hit the ball **hard**.	(adverb)

If you aren't sure if an adjective has a corresponding adverb form, use the **dictionary**.

Examples:	pretty	prettily
	ugly	ugily

However, for some words such as *silky* no adverb is given.

VERBS

Reviewing Linking Verbs

Directions: Write **L** in the space if the verb is on the linking verb list.

1. _____ to stop

2. _L_ to become

3. _L_ to sound

4. _L_ to eat

5. _L_ to taste

6. _L_ to grow

7. _L_ to go

8. _L_ to be

9. _L_ to think

10. _L_ to feel

11. _L_ to seem

12. _L_ to stay

13. _____ to watch

14. _L_ to look

15. _L_ to appear

16. _____ to break

17. _____ to grab

18. _L_ to remain

60

Some verbs can be used **either** as a linking verb **or** as an action verb. If you aren't sure, do the steps you practiced earlier:

1. Think about your list of linking verbs. Is the verb on that list? If it is not on the list, don't mark it as linking.

2. If the verb is on the linking verb list, write a form of _to be_ above the verb. _Is, am, are, was,_ or _were_ usually works well.

3. Read the sentence, inserting the form of _to be_. If the meaning of the sentence is not changed, the verb usually is linking.

Examples: ____ We <u>listened</u> carefully.   _Listened_ is not on the list.

                      is

        __L__ This shirt <u>feels</u> damp.   _To feel_ is on the list. Place a form of _to be_ above it.

                  was

        ____ The baby <u>grew</u> rapidly.

To grow is on the list. Place a form of _to be_ above it. **The baby was rapidly** makes no sense. _Grew_ in this sentence is an action verb.

❧❧❧❧❧❧❧❧❧❧❧❧❧❧❧❧❧❧❧❧❧❧

Directions: Write **L** in the space if the verb is linking. <u>Suggestion</u>:   Place a form of _to be_ above each verb to help determine if the verb is linking.

1. __L__ The crowd <u>remained</u> calm.

2. __L__ Your answers ^{is} <u>appear</u> correct.

3. __L__ A bolt ^{is} <u>lay</u> on the floor.

4. __L__ The children ^{is} <u>grew</u> restless.

5. __L__ This fabric ^{is} <u>looks</u> wrinkled.

6. __L__ Your buzzers ^{is} <u>sounded</u> loud.

7. _____ The gardener <u>smelled</u> the rose.

8. __L__ Her grandfather ^{is} <u>seems</u> nice.

Directions: Delete any prepositional phrases. Underline the subject once.
Write **L** in the space if the verb is linking.

Examples: ____   We <u>talked</u> together.   *Talked* is not on the list.

is

L   She <u>seems</u> upset.   *To seem* is on the list. Place a
form of *to be* above it.

was

____   A <u>clown</u> <u>appeared</u> suddenly.

To appear is on the list. Place a form of *to be* above it. **A clown
was suddenly** makes no sense. *Appeared* in this sentence is
not a linking verb.

1.   **L**   The <u>siren</u> <u>sounded</u> shrill.   *was*

2.   **L**   <u>He</u> <u>feels</u> slightly ill ~~after a race.~~   *is*

3.   **L**   <u>Broccoli</u> <u>tastes</u> good.   *is*

4.   **L**   Our <u>horses</u> <u>seem</u> energetic today.   *is*

5.   **L**   Their <u>sister</u> <u>appeared</u> nervous.   *is*

6.   **X** *you* <u>Tate</u> <u>tasted</u> the noodles.

7.   **X**   <u>Leah</u> <u>removed</u> the top ~~of the paint can.~~

8.   **X**   My <u>eyes</u> ~~in that picture~~ <u>look</u> odd.

9.   **L**   A <u>bellman</u> <u>became</u> confused ~~about the lady's luggage.~~   *was*

10.   **L**   Those barbecued <u>ribs</u> <u>smelled</u> delicious.   *are*

11.   **L**   <u>I</u> <u>am</u> very sleepy.   *was*

12.   **X**   <u>Chase</u> <u>washed</u> suds ~~off his hands.~~

13.   **L**   The <u>weather</u> <u>stayed</u> cold ~~until April.~~   *was*

14.   **L**   ~~During the dance,~~ <u>dessert</u> <u>remained</u> ~~on the table for two hours.~~   *was*

62

*2014
march* ©→

LINKING VERBS

Predicate Adjectives:

Do you remember that a linking verb actually joins or links the subject of the sentence with another word? Often, the word linked to the subject is an adjective, a describing word.

The <u>complete predicate</u> of a sentence **begins with the verb** and usually goes to the end of a sentence.

Example: Kami's stew **<u>tastes</u> salty**.

My cousin **<u>runs</u> fast in relay races**.

If the sentence is **interrogative** (a question), change the sentence to a statement before determining the complete predicate.

Example: Is this chicken spicy?

This chicken **<u>is</u> spicy**.   *Is spicy* is the complete predicate.

A **predicate adjective** (P.A.) is a describing word that happens **after the verb** and goes back to **describe the subject** of a sentence. Look at the last sentence.

P.A.

This <u>chicken</u> <u>is</u> spicy.

Spicy occurs after the verb (in the predicate). *Spicy* goes back to describe the subject, *chicken*. You can say, ***spicy chicken***. Spicy is called a predicate adjective. We label a predicate adjective with the letters, <u>P.A.</u>

<u>For a word to be a predicate adjective, it must:</u>
1.   <u>Be in a sentence containing a **linking verb**</u>.
2.   <u>Be in the **predicate** (after the verb)</u>.
3.   **<u>Describe the subject</u>** of the sentence.

P.A.

Examples: Your <u>decorations</u> <u>look</u> good.   *good decorations*

P.A.

~~After playing in the mud~~, my <u>dogs</u> <u>were</u> dirty.   *dirty dogs*

63

Note that we shall continue to cross out prepositional phrases. *A predicate adjective won't be in a prepositional phrase.*

Be sure to follow the rules for finding a predicate adjective. <u>First, look to see if the verb is on your linking verb list.</u> Read the following sentence.

Before the prom, the young man gave a pink corsage to his date.

<u>Find the subject and the verb</u>. Start by deleting prepositional phrases.

~~Before the prom,~~ the young <u>man</u> <u>gave</u> a pink corsage ~~to his date~~.

Note that the verb is *gave*.

    a.   *Gave* is not on the linking verb list.

    b.   Therefore, *pink* can't possibly be a predicate adjective.

    c.   You can also see that <u>*pink*</u> describes *corsage*, not the *man*.

Compound Predicate Adjectives:

More than one predicate adjective may appear in a sentence.

                                             P.A.   P.A.

Examples: Your <u>hair</u> <u>seems</u> soft and shiny.   *soft hair*
                                                  shiny hair

                                      P.A.   P.A.

Chan's <u>fingers</u> <u>are</u> long and slender.   *long fingers*
                                                slender fingers

    ᵔᵔᵔᵔᵔᵔᵔᵔᵔᵔᵔᵔᵔᵔᵔᵔᵔᵔᵔᵔᵔᵔ

*Remember: To check if the verb is linking, insert a form of <u>to be</u> for the verb. If you can do so and not change the meaning of the sentence, the verb generally will be a linking verb.

                                  was

His <u>decision</u> <u>remained</u> final.

64

Name Amanda Trumblee

Date 3/31/14

A. Directions: Look at the verb in the sentence. Place an **X** in the blank of the sentence that has a linking verb.

Remember: Write *is, am, are, was,* or *were* above the verb to help you.

1. ☒   You look relaxed.   *are*

      _____   My friend <u>looks</u> for caves.

2. _____   Marla <u>tasted</u> her soup.

      ☒   This frosting <u>tastes</u> sugary.   *is*

3. ☒   I <u>grew</u> excited about that.   *am*

      _____   A cactus <u>will grow</u> there.

4. _____   She <u>will remain</u> silent.

      ☒   The captain <u>remained</u> on board.   *is*

B. Directions: Cross out any prepositional phrases. Underline the subject once and the verb or verb phrase twice. Label any predicate adjective – **P.A.**

1. His <u>directions</u> <u>were</u> <u>correct</u>.   *P.A.*

2. These knife <u>blades</u> <u>seem</u> <u>blunt</u>.   *P.A.*

3. The garage <u>cabinets</u> <u>are</u> ~~too wide~~.

4. One <u>house</u> ~~on Willow Lane~~ <u>is</u> <u>expensive</u>.   *P.A*

5. This <u>pasta</u> <u>tastes</u> very <u>stale</u>.   *P.A.*

6. Their <u>cellar</u> <u>smells</u> <u>musty</u>.   *P.A.*

7. <u>You</u> <u>appear</u> <u>happy</u> ~~about your decision~~.   *P.A.*

8. <u>Many</u> ~~of the students~~ <u>remained</u> <u>noisy</u> ~~after the bell~~.   *P.A.*

9. These floral coffee <u>cups</u> <u>will look</u> <u>unusual</u> ~~beside checked plates~~.   *P.A.*

10. Their <u>grandparents</u> <u>become</u> <u>energetic</u> ~~after exercise class~~.   *P.A.*

11. Her new <u>sunglasses</u> <u>are</u> <u>plastic</u> ~~with rhinestones~~.   *P.A.*

65

Subject-Verb Agreement

To understand this concept, you need to understand the difference between singular and plural.

Singular means one.   Example: That **dog** sneezes.   (one dog)

కొ⃯కొ⃯కొ⃯కొ⃯కొ⃯కొ⃯కొ⃯కొ⃯కొ⃯కొ⃯కొ⃯కొ⃯కొ⃯కొ⃯

If the subject of a sentence is singular (only one), the verb must be singular.

Most verbs simply add _s_ (or _es_) to the verb in present tense (present time).
        Examples: My <u>gerbil</u> run**s**.   (one gerbil)

                Mr. Lua teach**es** at a college.   (one man)

The pronouns, _I_ and _you_, will not add _s_.   <u>I</u> **like** carrots. <u>You</u> **like** carrots.

కొ⃯కొ⃯కొ⃯కొ⃯కొ⃯కొ⃯కొ⃯కొ⃯కొ⃯కొ⃯కొ⃯కొ⃯కొ⃯కొ⃯

English can be confusing. Some irregular verbs have their own patterns for forming the present tense. One that is used frequently is _to be_:
        Examples: <u>I</u> **am** in training.

                ಹNote that _am_ is used with _I_.)

        One <u>woman</u> **is** in training.

                ಹNote a singular form of _to be_: **is**.

        <u>You</u> **are** the first to finish.

                ಹNote that _are_ is used with **you**.

        <u>Manny</u> and <u>Dakota</u> **are** quiet.   They **are** quiet.

                ಹNote that _are_ is used with a plural subject.

66

Remember: When using a singular subject, most verbs simply add <u>s</u> (or <u>es</u>) to the verb in the present tense (present time).

Examples: A <u>firefly</u> glow**s**.

<u>He</u> watch**es** baseball on television.

However, the pronouns, *you* and *I*, will not add *s*.   <u>I</u> want a video. <u>You</u> want a video.

Remember: Some irregular verbs have their own patterns for forming the present tense. One used frequently is *to be*.

Examples: <u>I</u> **am** a nurse.
That football <u>player</u> **is** in training.
<u>You</u> **are** angry.

᪣᪣᪣᪣᪣᪣᪣᪣᪣᪣᪣᪣᪣᪣᪣᪣᪣᪣᪣᪣᪣

Directions: Delete prepositional phrases. Underline the subject once. Place two lines under the verb that agrees with the subject.

1. A <u>panther</u> (run, <u>runs</u>) fast.

2. <u>I</u> (<u>swish</u>, swishes) ~~with mouthwash~~.

3. The <u>child</u> ~~on the skates~~ (tie, <u>ties</u>) her shoestrings ~~by herself~~.

4. <u>She</u> (wash, <u>washes</u>) her motorcycle ~~before each ride~~.

5. <u>I</u> (<u>am</u>, is) the owner ~~of a new baby lamb~~.

6. One <u>lady</u> ~~in the fabric store~~ (<u>makes</u>, make) pillows.

7. This ~~daisy with orange petals~~ (close, <u>closes</u>) ~~at night~~.

8. Their <u>dog</u> (wear, <u>wears</u>) a ribbon ~~atop her head~~.

9. <u>You</u> (is, <u>are</u>) my best buddy.

10. One tennis <u>player</u> (<u>wins</u>, win) many trophies ~~for his team~~.

11. <u>Mindy</u> (fold, <u>folds</u>) clothes ~~at a laundry after school~~.

Subject-Verb Agreement with Singular Subjects

This is material that you have learned; however, a review will enhance learning.

Present Tense (time):

If the subject of a sentence is singular (one), the verb must be singular.

Add **s** (or **es**) to most verbs.

Example: That <u>dog</u> **sneezes**.   (one dog)

The pronouns, **I** and **you**, will **not add s**.

Examples: I **pick** berries in the summer.   You **pick** berries in the summer.

Some irregular verbs such as **to be**, change forms. (With the pronoun, **you**, **are** is used.)   Examples: I **am** an animal lover.

This <u>wand</u> **is** made of metal. (one wand)

<u>You</u> **are** smart!

❧❧❧❧❧❧❧❧❧❧❧❧❧❧❧❧❧❧❧❧

Subject-Verb Agreement with Plural Subjects

Present Tense (time):

If the subject of a sentence is plural (more than one), the verb must be plural.

Do **NOT** add **s** (or **es**).

Examples: Those <u>dogs</u> **bark** constantly.   (more than one dog)

Some <u>riders</u> **leave** the horse trail. (more than one rider)

Some irregular verbs such as **to be** change forms.

Example: Several <u>seashells</u> **are** very pretty.

A **compound subject** joined by **and** requires that the verb **not** add the **s** (or **es**), unless it is a special verb that follows its own pattern.

Examples: <u>Beth</u> and <u>Tim</u> **go** to Aspen in the winter.
             compound subject

After sundown, <u>Tess</u> and <u>I</u> **play** hide-and-seek.
             compound subject

68

When using a singular subject, most verbs simply add s (or es) to the verb in present tense (present time).
          Example: My <u>sister</u> **uses** gel ~~on her hair~~.

~~However, the pronoun, *I*, will not add *s*.~~   I **use** gel.   <u>You</u> **use** gel.

Remember: Some irregular verbs have their own patterns for forming the present tense. One used frequently is *to be*:   <u>She</u> **is** a nurses' helper.

When using a plural subject, most verbs won't end in s (or es) in present tense.
          Example: Some <u>teams</u> **win** often.

ஃ௸ஃ௸ஃ௸ஃ௸ஃ௸ஃ௸ஃ௸ஃ௸ஃ௸ஃ௸ஃ௸ஃ௸

Directions: Delete prepositional phrases. Underline the subject once. Place
                two lines under the verb that agrees with the subject.

1.   Some fifth grade students (makes, make) beaded bracelets.

2.   Chessa (mix, mixes) ice cream with applesauce.

3.   He and his friends (sing, sings) without guitars.

4.   That photographer (take, takes) pictures after dark.

5.   The lady on stage (model, models) for a clothing store.

6.   My uncle (butters, butter) toast on both sides.

7.   Jack and she (is, are) advisors to the president.

8.   Loni (kiss, kisses) her new baby under his toes.

9.   Several dogs (chase, chases) balls in the park each Sunday.

10.   That gymnast (perform, performs) during half-time shows.

11.   Mom and Dad (play, plays) soccer on a parents' team.

12.   Tailors at that men's shop (alters, alter) cuffs.

13.   One of the newswomen (talk, talks) about stocks.

Name_____   **VERBS**

Date__9/10/14_____   **Don't and Doesn't**

Some people have a problem with using <u>doesn't</u> and <u>don't</u>.

Use <u>does</u> (<u>doesn't</u>) with *he, she,* and other *singular* subjects.
         Examples: <u>He</u> <u>does</u>n't like to play pool.
                      <u>She</u> <u>does</u>n't want to stand on her head.
                      That <u>giraffe</u> <u>does</u>n't have many spots.

Use <u>do</u> (<u>don't</u>) with the pronouns, *I* and *you*.   <u>I</u> <u>do</u>n't chase bunnies.
                                            <u>You</u> <u>do</u>n't seem to understand.

Use <u>do</u> (<u>don't</u>) with plural subjects.   Some <u>athletes</u> <u>do</u>n't eat sweets.
                                     <u>Peter</u> and <u>Leah</u> <u>do</u>n't carry their lunch.
                                     <u>We</u> <u>do</u>n't need more straws.

🐎🐎🐎🐎🐎🐎🐎🐎🐎🐎🐎🐎🐎🐎🐎🐎🐎🐎🐎🐎🐎

A.   Directions: Underline the subject once.   Circle the correct word.

1.   He (doesn't, don't) shop here.

2.   Mom and my aunt (doesn't, don't) shop here.

3.   My friends (doesn't, don't) bother me.

4.   She (don't, doesn't) bother me.

🐎🐎🐎🐎🐎🐎🐎🐎🐎🐎🐎

B.   Directions: Underline the subject once.   Circle the correct word.

1.   I (doesn't, don't) want any gravy.

2.   We (doesn't, don't) gossip.

3.   That seal (don't, doesn't) sleep often.

4.   My one shoe (don't, doesn't) fit properly.

5.   Your drink (doesn't, don't) look cold.

6.   My doctor (don't, doesn't) take credit cards.

7.   Marco and his sister (doesn't, don't) hike there.

70

Some people have a problem with using doesn't and don't.

Use does (doesn't) with _he, she_, and other _singular_ subjects.
        Examples: He doesn't dance.
                      She doesn't whistle.
                      My grandpa doesn't eat spinach.

Use do (don't) with the pronouns, _I_ and _you_.   I don't yell.
                                            You don't have to reply.

Use do (don't) with plural subjects.   My parents don't need help.
                                    His knees and ankles don't hurt today.
                                    They don't plant a garden.

A. Directions: Underline the subject once. Circle the correct word. (Be sure
                      to cross out the prepositional phrase in number 12.)

1. That crime (doesn't, don't) occur often.

2. I (don't, doesn't) want this.

3. He (don't, doesn't) remember my name.

4. Her cat and kittens (don't, doesn't) go outside.

5. That penquin (don't, doesn't) waddle fast.

6. We (doesn't, don't) have a pool.

7. Your idea (don't, doesn't) sound silly.

8. (Don't, Doesn't) clams live long lives?

9. Brian's father (don't, doesn't) fish.

10. She usually (don't, doesn't) take a day off.

11. The lifeguard (doesn't, don't) talk often.

12. One of their friends (doesn't, don't) wash his own car.

A transitive verb has a direct object.
Remember: A direct object occurs after the verb and receives the action of the verb.
                              D.O.
          Example: I <u>threw</u> a ball.

A transitive verb has a direct object.   I <u>threw</u> a ball.   ***Threw*** is a transitive verb here.

It's easy to remember this by using the initials, **D.O.T.**   **D**irect **O**bject = **T**ransitive

If the sentence **does not contain a direct object**, the verb is ***intransitive***.

🪱🪱🪱🪱🪱🪱🪱🪱🪱🪱🪱🪱🪱🪱🪱🪱🪱🪱🪱🪱🪱

A.   Directions: Underline the subject once and the verb or verb phrase twice.
                            Label the direct object.

1.   I spilled my milk.   4.   Rena shipped a package.

2.   His mom makes quilts.   5.   Brad plays the trombone.

3.   You told the truth.   6.   A waiter took our order.

🪱🪱🪱🪱🪱🪱🪱🪱🪱🪱🪱🪱🪱

B.   Directions: Underline the subject once and the verb or verb phrase twice.
                            Label the direct object – **D.O.** If the sentence is transitive, write
                            T in the blank. If the sentence is intransitive, write **I** in the blank.

1.   This light bulb no longer works.   _____

2.   A security guard searched my purse.   _____

3.   Ms. Yazzie creates beautiful Navajo rugs.   _____

4.   A sailor checked his email twice.   _____

5.   They are not going now.   _____

6.   Shawn starts his computer early.   _____

7.   Their best friend is a social worker.   _____

8.   A salesperson handed us free samples.   _____ .

72

A. **The Verb, *To Be*:**
    Directions: Fill in the blank with the correct form of the infinitive, *to be*.

1. Right now, I _____ here.

2. You _____ now correct.

3. He _____ always funny.

4. Yesterday, the children _____ noisy.

5. Mr. Hanks _____ here tomorrow.

❦❦❦❦❦❦❦❦❦❦❦

B. **Contractions:**
    Directions: Write the contraction.

1. cannot - _____   6. they are - _____

2. he is - _____   7. where is - _____

3. have not - _____   8. is not - _____

4. who is - _____   9. should not - _____

5. did not - _____   10. he will - _____

❦❦❦❦❦❦❦❦❦❦❦

C. **You're/Your, It's/Its, and They're/Their/There:**
    Directions: Circle the correct word.

1. The crafters placed (they're, their, there) carved ducks on display.

2. After you paint (you're, your) room, you may need a new bedspread.

3. The newly born colt stood on (it's, its) wobbly legs.

4. Do you know if (they're, their, there) ready for the outing?

5. I want a muffin if (it's, its) not moldy.

6. (They're, Their, There) may be an election soon.   73

D. **Auxiliary (Helping) Verbs:**
Directions: Write the 23 helping verbs.

1. d_____	7. m_____	13. c_____	19. w_____
2. d_____	8. m_____	14. s_____	20. w_____
3. d_____	9. m_____	15. w_____	21. b_____
4. h_____	10. c_____	16. i_____	22. b_____
5. h_____	11. s_____	17. a_____	23. b_____
6. h_____	12. w_____	18. a_____	

E. **Irregular Verbs:**
Directions: Underline the subject once and the correct verb phrase twice.

1. The boy has (chose, chosen) a striped wallpaper.

2. They might have (went, gone) early.

3. Tim should have (driven, drove) his pick-up truck.

4. Their baby had (lain, laid) quietly.

5. I could have (ran, run) farther.

F. **Subjects, Verbs, and Direct Objects:**
Directions: Cross out any prepositional phrases. Underline the
subject once and the verb/verb phrase twice. Label any
direct object – **D.O.**

1. A gum wrapper is lying on the floor.

2. I should have written my message.

3. During a flood, those deer must have moved to higher ground.

4. Could you have lost your wallet at the mall?

5. The hammer was not with the other tools.

74

6. Will Josh slice the turkey at Thanksgiving?

7. We didn't have any coins for a bus ride.

8. Did Neema and you suggest a plan?

9. One of the bingo players coughed and left the room.

10. Do not close the door.

ತ್ತ-ತ್ತ-ತ್ತ-ತ್ತ-ತ್ತ-ತ್ತ-ತ್ತ-ತ್ತ-ತ್ತ-ತ್ತ-ತ್ತ-ತ್ತ

G. **Sit/Set, Lie/Lay, and Rise/Raise:**
   Directions: Delete any prepositional phrases. Underline the
               subject once and the verb/verb phrase twice. Label
               any direct object-**D.O.**

1. I might (sit, set) in the last row.

2. You must have (lay, laid) your paper under your notebook.

3. He (rose, raised) his arm in warning.

4. The patient (laid, lay) on a stretcher.

5. Has Sally (set, sat) her umbrella by her front door?

ತ್ತ-ತ್ತ-ತ್ತ-ತ್ತ-ತ್ತ-ತ್ತ-ತ್ತ-ತ್ತ-ತ್ತ-ತ್ತ-ತ್ತ-ತ್ತ

H. **Tenses:**
   Directions: Underline the subject once and the verb or verb
                phrase twice. Write the tense (*present, past,* or *future*).

1. _____ He bought sandals yesterday.

2. _____ My foot aches.

3. _____ Will you finish later?

4. _____ Tally dreams often.

5. _____ The black Labrador rescued his owner.

I. Linking Verbs:

Directions: Write the linking verbs.

1. to _____   8. to _____   c. _____

2. to _____   9. to _____   d. _____

3. to _____   10. to _____   e. _____

4. to _____   11. to _____   f. _____

5. to _____   12. to _____   g. _____

6. to_____   a. _____   h. _____

7. to _____   b. _____

❧❧❧❧❧❧❧❧❧❧❧❧❧

J. Action Verb or Linking Verb?:

Directions: Write **A** if the verb is action; write **L** if the verb is linking.

1. _____   I <u>sneezed</u>.   4. _____   He <u>looked</u> at his map.

2. _____   My voice <u>sounds</u> raspy.   5. _____   This apple <u>tastes</u> tart.

3. _____   Our goat <u>bleated</u>.   6. _____   A cat <u>appeared</u> in the alley.

❧❧❧❧❧❧❧❧❧❧❧❧❧

K. Linking Verbs and Predicate Adjectives:

Directions: Write **L** in the space if the verb is linking. Place a form of *to be* above each verb to help determine if the verb is linking.

Remember: Try placing *is, am, are, was,* or *were* in place of the verb. If the meaning of the sentence does not change, the verb is probably linking.

1. _____   She <u>remained</u> quiet.

2. _____   Your ideas <u>sound</u> great.

3. _____   We <u>climbed</u> a tower in Paris.

76

4. _____ That weed <u>grows</u> very rapidly.

5. _____ Your spiced chicken <u>tastes</u> delicious.

6. _____ Water <u>poured</u> into the gulley.

7. _____ Those men <u>became</u> business partners.

🙖🙖🙖🙖🙖🙖🙖🙖🙖🙖🙖🙖

L. Linking Verbs and Predicate Adjectives:
    Directions: Delete any prepositional phrases. Underline the subject once and the verb twice. Label any predicate adjective – **P.A.**

1. That oak chest with white knobs is old.

2. Your dog's ears seem small for his body size.

3. The corn in those fields looks very dry.

4. Blueberries taste good on cereal.

🙖🙖🙖🙖🙖🙖🙖🙖🙖🙖🙖🙖

M. Subject-Verb Agreement:
    Directions: Delete any prepositional phrases. Underline the subject once. Underline the verb or verb phrase that agrees with the subject twice.

1. A mason (places, place) bricks for a wall.

2. These dents (looks, look) mild.

3. A shepherd (lead, leads) his sheep.

4. Ham and eggs (are, is) his favorite breakfast.

5. Jim (does(n't), do(n't)) work near the new shopping center.

6. Many parents (talk, talks) with school counselor.

7. Little beads (hang, hangs) from the floral lampshade.

8. Kit and Rana (rides, ride) the bus each day.

9. We (deliver, delivers) newspapers on our street.

10. One of the baskets (was, were) sold.

11. Clerks at the photo counter (checks, check) pictures.

12. Those volunteers (cover, covers) old tins with fabric.

13. The girls' mother (drink, drinks) green tea.

14. He (does[n't]), do[n't]) want a bath.

இஇஇஇஇஇஇஇஇஇஇஇஇ

N. Transitive and Intransitive Verbs:

Directions: Cross out any prepositional phrases. Underline the subject once and the verb or verb phrase twice. Label any direct object – **D.O.** Write **T** if the verb is transitive; write **I** if the verb is intransitive.

Remember: A transitive verb will have a direct object.
D.O.T. = Direct **O**bject **- T**ransitive

1. You may grill chicken for dinner.   _____

2. These jelly beans are sticky.   _____

3. I collect baseball cards.   _____

4. A pigeon landed by a fountain in the park. _____

5. The men at the market sell vegetables.   _____

6. Dry this sweater on a low setting.   _____

Name_____

Date___9/20/14_____

A. List of Prepositions:

Directions: Write the prepositions by adding missing letters.

A's

1. _ b _ u t

2. _ b o _ _

3. _ _ r _ _ s

4. _ _ t _ r

5. _ g _ i _ _ t

6. _ l _ n _

7. _ m _ d

8. _ m _ _ g

9. _ r _ _ n d

10. a _

11. a _ _ p

B's

12. _ _ f _ r e

13. _ e _ _ n d

14. _ _ l o _

15. _ e n _ _ _ h

16. _ e s _ d _

17. _ e t w _ _ n

18. _ e _ o _ d

19. _ u _ (meaning except)

20. _ y

C's

21. c _ n c _ r _ i _ _

D's

22. _ o _ n

23. _ _ r _ _ g

E's

24. _ _ c _ _ t

F's

25. _ o _

26. _ _ _ m

I's

27. _ n

28. _ n s _ _ _

29. _ n _ _

L's

30. _ i _ _

N's

31. _ e _ r

O's

32. _ f

33. _ _ f

34. _ n

35. _ n _ o

36. _ _ t

37. _ _ _ s i _ e

38. _ _ e r

P's

39. _ a _ t

R's

40. _ e g _ r _ _ n g

S's

41. _ _ _ c e

T's

42. _ _ r _ u _ h

43. _ h _ o _ _ h _ u t

44. _ o

45. _ o _ _ _ d

U's

46. _ n _ _ r

47. _ n d _ r n _ _ t h

48. _ n _ _ l

49. u _

50. _ _ o n

W's

51. _ _ t _

52. _ _ _ h i _

53. _ _ t _ _ u _

B. **Subject/Verb:**
   Directions: Cross out any prepositional phrases. Underline the subject once
   and the verb twice.

1. A wet mop lay on the damp floor.

2. Your dirty socks are in the hamper.

3. Winds from the east swept through the valley.

4. The man at the carnival served ice cream.

C. **Verb Phrases:**
   Directions: Cross out any prepositional phrases. Underline the subject once
   and the verb phrase twice.

1. Your ice cream cone is dripping.

2. The race must have begun at noon.

3. Did Ryan take his dog with him to the park?

D. **Compound Objects of the Preposition:**
   Directions: Cross out any prepositional phrases. Underline the subject once
   and the verb twice.

1. A teacher sat between Juan and his sister.

2. This report about snakes and other reptiles is long.

3. One camel spit at its owner and us.

E. **Compound Subjects:**
   Directions: Cross out any prepositional phrases. Underline the subject once
   and the verb twice.

1. Joy and her sister live near a large pond.

2. The old mill and waterwheel are around this bend in the road.

80

F. **Compound Verbs:**
    Directions: Cross out any prepositional phrases. Underline the subject once
                  and the verb twice.

1. During exercise class, I stopped and rested for five minutes.

2. Several tourists walked across the bridge and went inside the castle.

G. **Imperative Sentences:**
    Directions: Cross out any prepositional phrases. Underline the subject once
                  and the verb twice.

1. Go without us.

2. Wait until Saturday.

3. Prop this shovel against the wall.

H. **Infinitives:**
    Directions: Cross out any prepositional phrases. Place parentheses ( )
                  around any infinitive. Underline the subject once and the verb
                  twice.

1. Parker likes to play at a playground near her home.

2. Uncle Don wants to go on a fishing trip.

3. Everyone except the man with a broken leg decided to wade in the stream.

I. **Preposition or Adverb?:**
    Directions: Cross out any prepositional phrases. Underline the subject once
                  and the verb twice. Write **A** if the boldfaced word is an adverb.
                  Write **P** if the boldfaced word is a preposition that begins a
                  prepositional phrase.

1. _____   Their ferrets run **around**.
2. _____   Their ferrets run **around** their home.

3. _____   A bear came **near**.
4. _____   A bear came **near** our camp.

J. **Verb Phrases and *Not*:**
    Directions: Cross out any prepositional phrases. Box *not* or *n't*.
                  Underline the subject once and the verb twice.

1.   You may not go beyond that blue dot.

2.   I should not have ridden along the busy highway.

3.   Some baseball fans weren't staying through the last inning.

K. **General Review:**
    Directions: Cross out any prepositional phrases. Underline the subject
                  once and the verb or verb phrase twice.

           Example: Those <u>tadpoles</u> <u>are swimming</u> ~~in a circle~~.

1.   They have placed twenty candles atop his birthday cake.

2.   During high winds, the boat pulled into the harbor.

3.   Our team decided to stay inside the gym for practice.

4.   Several mothers and toddlers met after a puppet show.

5.   The attorney answers her calls throughout the day.

6.   I haven't seen him since last Friday.

7.   Five dimes fell off the table and onto a checked sofa.

8.   We sit by a fountain before school.

9.   Mary put a hat with a huge feather upon her head and laughed.

10.   One of the artists painted a box within a box.

11.   A man with red suspenders tossed a hay bale into his truck.

12.   Did her dog trot toward an open door?

CONCRETE AND ABSTRACT NOUNS

Do you remember the definition of a noun?

A noun names a person, a place, or a thing.

We will add *idea* to this definition.

A noun names a person, a place, a thing, or an idea.

Examples:	person	-	girl or Tara
	place	-	park or Idaho
	thing	-	spoon or crane
	idea	-	beauty or forgiveness

ळ्

Nouns can be concrete or abstract.

A. Concrete Nouns:

Concrete nouns can be seen.

Examples: drum

house

moon

skunk

Concrete nouns are made up of atoms. At first, air may not seem concrete. However, using high-powered equipment, you can see atoms.

B. Abstract Nouns:

Abstract nouns cannot be seen.

Examples: love

gentleness

eternity

anger

Directions: Write **C** in the blank if the noun is concrete and **A** if it is abstract.

1. _____   tub

2. _____   man

3. _____   trust

4. _____   toothpaste

5. _____   hatred

6. _____   steel

7. _____   fright

8. _____   faucet

9. _____   bacon

10. _____   laughter

11. _____   bulldozer

12. _____   stubborness

13. _____   rafter

14. _____   rattlesnake

15. _____   intelligence

16. _____   happiness

17. _____   justice

18. _____   snack

A noun names a person, place, thing, or idea.

Two types are **common nouns** and **proper nouns**.

    A. Common nouns do not name a specific person, place, or thing.
        Examples: boy   day   planet   dog

Sometimes, a common noun can be classified into types. Types are still common nouns and are not capitalized.
        Example: dog   -   collie
However, if part of a type names a specific place, capitalize that place.
        Examples: **F**rench poodle   (place – France)
                    Bermuda grass   (place – Bermuda)

    B. Proper nouns name a specific person, place, or thing. Capitalize any proper noun.

	Common	**Proper**
Examples:	boy	**D**avid
	day	**M**onday
	planet	**M**ars
	dog	**V**elvet

                        ରୈ ରୈ ରୈ ରୈ ରୈ ରୈ ରୈ ରୈ ରୈ ରୈ

Directions: Write **C** if the noun is common and **P** if the noun is proper.

1. ___	person	11. ___	ranch	21. ___	animal
2. ___	Bar Harbor	12. ___	party	22. ___	horse
3. ___	Sara	13. ___	Mr. Sands	23. ___	Mt. Hood
4. ___	partner	14. ___	state	24. ___	doctor
5. ___	Vermont	15. ___	holiday	25. ___	Hawaii
6. ___	January	16. ___	restaurant	26. ___	waitress
7. ___	month	17. ___	mountain	27. ___	dock
8. ___	building	18. ___	Dr. Small	28. ___	flower
9. ___	club	19. ___	suburb	29. ___	daisy
10. ___	Dell Bank	20. ___	island	30. ___	Thanksgiving

Common nouns do not name a specific person, place, or thing.
> Examples: neck   ticket   heart   glue

Sometimes, a common noun can be classified into types. Types are still common nouns and are not capitalized.

Common	**Type**	**Proper**
girl	teenager	Lani
horse	mare	Lady Jewel

However, if part of a type names a specific place, capitalize that place.
>   dog   shepherd   **N**inja
> ▼
>   **G**erman shepherd   (place – Germany)

Proper nouns name a specific person, place, or thing. Capitalize any proper noun.

Common	**Proper**
month	**O**ctober

Directions: Write a common noun in Column A, a type of the common noun in Column B, and a proper noun that relates to the common noun in Column C.

Column A COMMON NOUN	**Column B** TYPE (COMMON NOUN)	**Column C** PROPER NOUN
1. __place__	_____	_____
2. __horse__	_____	_____
3. __business__	_____	_____
4. __waterform__	_____	_____
5. __residence__	_____	_____
6. __landform__	_____	_____
7. __book__	_____	_____

Name_____

Date____9/30/14_____

You have learned that **a noun names a person, place, thing, or idea.**

Sometimes, the same word will be a noun in one sentence and an adjective (describing word) in another sentence.

Examples: A. He planted a **bean** in this cup.

Bean is a noun in this sentence.

B. I don't like this **bean** salad.   ___*bean salad*___

Bean is an adjective in this sentence because it describes salad.

Directions: On the line provided, write **N** if the boldfaced word serves as a noun and **A** if the word serves as an adjective (describing word). If your answer is **A**, write the adjective and the word it modifies.

1. _____ I like your **clothes**. _____

2. _____ A **clothes** brush is lying on the bed. _____

3. _____ This **picture** frame is broken. _____

4. _____ Our **picture** appeared in the newspaper. _____

5. _____ We attended a **beauty** pageant. _____

6. _____ **Beauty** in nature is all around us. _____

7. _____ He needs a **water** bottle for his backpack. _____

8. _____ I need **water** for my dog's dish. _____

9. _____ Jana wants an **egg** sandwich. _____

10. _____ May I please have an **egg** with cheese? _____

11. _____ You may use my **telephone** to make a call. _____

12. _____ There are no **telephone** wires in their area. _____

The same word may serve as a noun in one sentence and as an adjective (describing word) in another sentence.

Example: I put **gas** in my car.   (noun)

They cook on a **gas** range.   _gas_ range   (adjective)

Directions: Write a sentence using the boldfaced word as a noun in Part A and as an adjective in Part B. In Part B, draw an arrow from your word to what it describes.

1. **window**

    A. _____

    B. _____

2. **apple**

    A. _____

    B. _____

3. **beach**

    A. _____

    B. _____

4. **football**

    A. _____

    B. _____

5. **nose**

    A. _____

    B. _____

PLURAL NOUNS:

Plural means more than one.

    Singular: (one) dime   **Plural:** (many) dimes

Notice that an apostrophe (') is **not** used when forming the plural.

Rule A: Most nouns simply add **s** to form the plural.

	Examples:	banan**A**	-	banana**s**
		cur**B**	-	curb**s**
		tarma**C**	-	tarmac**s**
		fa**D**	-	fad**s**
		dimpl**E**	-	dimple**s**
		puf**F**	-	puff**s**
		ru**G**	-	rug**s**
		pat**H**	-	path**s**
		sk**I**	-	ski**s**
		bac**K**	-	back**s**
		dol**L**	-	doll**s**
		mo**M**	-	mom**s**
		ca**N**	-	can**s**

89

dri**P**	-	drip**s**
sta**R**	-	star**s**
do**T**	-	dot**s**
la**W**	-	law**s**

Note that the following letters are missing from the list:

J, O, Q, S, U, V, X, Y, and Z

J, Q, U, and *V?*

Most English words do not end in these letters.

However, we do have words that have been added to our language via a foreign language. For example, <u>luau</u> is from the Hawaiian language. This word, which means *party,* has become standard in our English language and simply adds **s** to form the plural.

What about *S*, *X*, and *Z?* These follow Rule B.

Rule B: Nouns ending in <u>**sh**</u>, <u>**ch**</u>, <u>**s**</u>, <u>**x**</u>, and <u>**z**</u> usually add *es* to form the plural.

cla**sh**	clash**es**
pat**ch**	patch**es**
dres**s**	dress**es**
bo**x**	box**es**
fiz**z**	fizz**es**

What about *O* and *Y?*

O and *Y* follow rules that you will learn later in this unit.

Name_____

Date_____

Directions: Write a noun that ends with the given letter or letters. Then, write the plural of that word.

1. _____ w - _____   10. _____ x - _____

2. _____ b - _____   11. _____ k - _____

3. _____ d - _____   12. _____ l - _____

4. _____ e - _____   13. _____ m - _____

5. _____ f - _____   14. _____ n - _____

6. _____ g - _____   15. _____ p - _____

7. _____ sh - _____   16. _____ r - _____

8. _____ ch - _____   17. _____ s - _____

9. _____ th - _____   18. _____ t - _____

෮෮෮෮෮෮෮෮෮෮෮෮෮෮෮෮෮෮෮෮෮෮෮෮෮෮෮෮෮෮

Directions: Circle any noun that adds **s** to form the plural; box any noun that adds **es** to form the plural.

1. spa   10. prison   19. fuzz   28. chorus

2. rib   11. due   20. foul   29. trick

3. tunic   12. swirl   21. wrench   30. replica

4. flood   13. inch   22. corral   31. hymn

5. flame   14. gash   23. tactic   32. gondola

6. flaw   15. iceberg   24. weight   33. legend

7. flush   16. color   25. process   34. caboose

8. fountain   17. cross   26. reflex   35. branch

9. brunch   18. target   27. mansion   36. germ

Singular means one.   Plural means more than one.

Rule A: Most nouns add _s_ to form the plural.

one garden	two garden**s**
one bolt	many bolt**s**

Rule B: Nouns ending in **sh**, **ch**, **s**, **x**, and **z** usually add _es_ to form the plural.

one bru**sh**	two brush**es**
one por**ch**	several porch**es**
one len**s**	three lens**es**
an apartment comple**x**	many apartment complex**es**
buz**z**	buzz**es**

ৼৼৼৼৼৼৼৼৼৼৼৼৼৼৼৼৼৼৼৼৼৼ

Directions: Write the plural of each noun.

1.   flash - _____

2.   eagle - _____

3.   fez - _____

4.   canvas - _____

5.   arrival - _____

6.   ranch - _____

7.   hostess - _____

8.   sauna - _____

9.   basic - _____

10.   circus - _____

Plural means more than one.

Rule C: Nouns ending in **<u>ay</u>**, **<u>ey</u>**, **<u>oy</u>**, and **<u>uy</u>** add **s** to form the plural.

one pathw**ay**	two pathway**s**
one all**ey**	many alley**s**
one dec**oy**	a few decoy**s**
one g**uy**	ten guy**s**

Rule D: Nouns ending in **<u>consonant + y</u>** change the **<u>y</u>** to **<u>i</u>** and add **es** to form the plural.

one pat**ty**	two patt**ies**
one cana**ry**	some canar**ies**
one dol**ly**	three doll**ies**
a ba**by**	bab**ies**

Remember: Consonants are *b, c, d, f, g, h, j, k, l, m, n, p, q, r, s, t, v, w, x,* and *z.*

ᏽᏽᏽᏽᏽᏽᏽᏽᏽᏽᏽᏽᏽᏽᏽᏽᏽᏽᏽᏽᏽ

Directions: Write the plural of each noun.

1. screenplay - _____

2. county - _____

3. country - _____

4. gulley - _____

5. buggy - _____

6. lobby - _____

7. alloy - _____

8. reply - _____

9. latchkey - _____

10. buy - _____

Plural means more than one.

Rule C: Nouns ending in **ay**, **ey**, **oy**, and **uy** add **s** to form the plural.

> w**ay**   way**s**
> k**ey**   key**s**
> t**oy**   toy**s**

Rule D: Nouns ending in **consonant + y** change the **y** to **i** and add **es** to form the plural.

> jet**ty**   jett**ies**
> la**dy**   lad**ies**
> c**ry**   cr**ies**

Directions: Place a check (✔) in the blank if you change **y** to **i** and add **es** to form the plural.

1. _____   battery

2. _____   holiday

3. _____   puppy

4. _____   ploy

5. _____   nanny

6. _____   bluejay

7. _____   dummy

8. _____   abbey

9. _____   story

10. _____   piggy

94

Plural means more than one.

Rule E: Some nouns ending in **o** add **s** to form the plural.

halo   halos
buffo   buffos

However, some nouns ending in **o** add **es** to form the plural.

tomato   tomatoes

Some nouns ending in **o** can add **s or es**.

USE A DICTIONARY TO DETERMINE THE CORRECT PLURAL ENDING!

If two plural endings are given, the first one is preferred. Use it.

Example: mango (man go) n. pl. es, s 1. The sweet orange-fleshed fruit of an Indian tree…

ぞぞぞぞぞぞぞぞぞぞぞぞぞぞぞぞぞぞぞぞ

Directions: Write the plural of each noun. If necessary, use a dictionary.

1.   patio - _____

2.   flamingo - _____

3.   bongo - _____

4.   dingo - _____

5.   alto - _____

6.   dodo - _____

7.   zero - _____

8.   pimento - _____

9.   bronco - _____

10.   motto - _____

Plural means more than one.

Rule F: Some nouns ending in **f** add **s** to form the plural.

cliff   cliff**s**

However, some nouns ending in **f** change the **f** to **v** and add **es** to form the plural.

loa**f**   loa**ves**

USE A DICTIONARY TO DETERMINE THE CORRECT PLURAL ENDING!

*If no "special" plural ending is stated, simply add **s** to form the plural.*

Directions: Write the plural of each noun. If necessary, use a dictionary.

1. cuff - _____

2. leaf - _____

3. bluff - _____

4. staff - _____

5. hoof - _____

6. whiff - _____

7. mastiff - _____

8. wharf - _____

9. reef - _____

10. elf - _____

11. muff - _____

Plural means more than one.

Rule G: Some nouns completely change to form the plural.

goose   geese

Some nouns that have entered our language from Latin will change
to form the plural.

medium (as in television)   media

USE A DICTIONARY TO DETERMINE THE CORRECT PLURAL ENDING!

Rule H: Some nouns do not change to form the plural.

deer   deer

Directions: Write the plural of each noun. If necessary, use a dictionary.

1. fungus - _____

2. moose - _____

3. mouse - _____

4. louse - _____

5. reindeer - _____

6. patriotism - _____

7. police - _____

8. craftsman - _____

9. woman - _____

10. elk - _____

Name_____   **NOUNS**

Date____|4_____   **Plurals**

A.   Directions: Write each plural noun. If necessary, use a dictionary.

1.   ceremony - _____

2.   coach - _____

3.   troop - _____

4.   cliff - _____

5.   circus - _____

6.   jury - _____

7.   value - _____

8.   trench - _____

B.   Directions: Circle the correct spelling of the plural form.

1.   fossils   fossiles

2.   ponys   ponies

3.   stairwaies   stairways

4.   furniture   furnitures

5.   studios   studioes

6.   datas   data

7.   swatches   swatchs

8.   jettys   jetties

9.   splashs   spashes

10.   halos   haloes

NOUN DETERMINERS are yellow lights. When you see one, slow down and see if a noun is following it. For example, **a** is a determiner. When you see **a** in a sentence, examine the words that follow it.

noun   noun   noun

Example: **A** fluffy white <u>cloud</u> in **the** <u>shape</u> of **a** <u>balloon</u> appeared.

Note that the noun may have another word or words in front of it: *A fluffy white* <u>cloud</u>

భ్రా భ్రా భ్రా భ్రా భ్రా భ్రా భ్రా భ్రా భ్రా భ్రా భ్రా భ్రా భ్రా భ్రా భ్రా భ్రా భ్రా భ్రా భ్రా

Classification of Determiners:

A. Articles: **A**, **an**, and **the** will come before a noun. As you have already learned, the noun may have another word in front of it.

         Examples: a <u>pebble</u>   an <u>ant</u>   the dark <u>woods</u>

B. Demonstratives: **This**, **that**, **these**, and **those** MAY come before a noun. However, sometimes they stand alone.

         Examples: this <u>photo</u>   that salad <u>fork</u>   these <u>clips</u>   those <u>bugs</u>

If **this**, **that**, **these**, or **those** does NOT have a person, place, thing, or idea following it (closely), it may stand alone and will not be a determiner.

         Examples: *This* is great!   (*This* stands alone and isn't a determiner here.)

                   I want *these*. (*These* stands alone and isn't a determiner here.)

C. Numbers: Numbers **MAY** signal a noun. Other words often come between a number and a noun.

           Examples: nine <u>players</u>   twenty-two baseball <u>games</u>

If a **number** does NOT have a person, place, thing, or idea following it (closely), it may stand alone and will not be a determiner:

         Examples: I'd like *two*, please.(*Two* stands alone and isn't a determiner here.)

D. Possessive Adjectives (also called possessive pronouns): **My, his, her, your, its, our, their**, and **whose** often signal a noun. Check to see if a noun naming a person, place, thing, or idea is following. *My, your, its, our, their,* and *whose* will usually be followed by a noun. <u>Check *her* carefully</u>.

         Examples: my <u>mom</u>   his <u>tongue</u>   her new <u>bike</u>   your <u>video</u>

                     its <u>wing</u>   our <u>aunts</u>   their ear <u>drum</u>   whose <u>idea</u>

Do you want to go with **her**?   (*Her* stands alone and is not a determiner.)

E. Possessive Nouns: Possessive nouns often signal other nouns. Possessive means ownership. Look for a word naming a person, place, thing, or idea after any possessive noun.   Examples: **Bill's** <u>wallet</u>   **girls'** tennis <u>match</u>

F. Indefinites: some, few, many, several, no, any* Indefinites can be determiners. When you see one of the above words, see if a noun follows it. Other words may occur between an indefinite and a noun.

         Examples: some cream <u>cheese</u> few <u>markers</u>   many <u>times</u>

                 several <u>talks</u>   no fresh <u>water</u>   any soft <u>pretzels</u>

An indefinite may stand alone. If it does, it is not a determiner.

         Examples: *Several* are going.

*There are others.   I'll take *several*.

Directions: Write the boldfaced determiner and the noun that it modifies
(goes over to) in the blank.

Example: **His** eye hurts.   ___**His eye**___

1.   **This** banjo is out of tune.   _____

2.   Do you have **an** excuse?   _____

3.   Tell me **your** funny story.   _____

4.   Kammi is selling **her** car.   _____

5.   **Ten** customers stood in line.   _____

6.   We like **those** oil paintings.   _____

7.   **Bonnie's** daughter is a pilot.   _____

8.   Bass were caught in **the** lake.   _____

9.   I think that **ten** people won the raffle.   _____

10.   **That** Navajo rug is valuable.   _____

11.   **Many** roads in **their** area are new.   _____

          _____

12.   Do you want to play **these** drums?   _____

13.   **Our** friend modeled **several** times.   _____

          _____

14.   I don't want **any** prunes.   _____

15.   That is **Lou's** grandmother.   _____

100

Name_____   **NOUNS**

Date_____   **Determiners**

Directions: Place a ✓ in the blank if the boldfaced word is a determiner. If the

word serves as a determiner, write the boldfaced word and the

noun that it modifies (goes over to) in the wide blank.

1. ___ She ordered **three** sandwiches.   _____

2. ___ The toddler is **three**.   _____

3. ___ I want to meet **her** mother.   _____

4. ___ We had to start without **her**.   _____

5. ___ Are **these** new?   _____

6. ___ **These** ideas are good ones.   _____

7. ___ **Many** were waiting in line.   _____

8. ___ **Many** students tried out for the play._____

9. ___ Todd bought **Tara's** pottery.   _____

10. ___ Is this **Tara's**?   _____

11. ___ He chose **those** for their wedding.   _____

12. ___ Please pick up **those** sticks.   _____

13. ___ We gave **several** to our friends.   _____

14. ___ They own **several** stocks.   _____

15. ___ **Few** need that surgery.   _____

16. ___ **Few** people decided to stay.   _____

Determiners:
A. **Articles:** **a, an, the**
B. **Demonstratives:** **this, that, those, these**
C. **Numbers:** (**one** block)
D. **Possessive Adjectives** (possessive pronouns)**:**
          my, his, her, your, its, our, their
E. **Possessive Nouns** (used as adjectives)**:** (**Bo's** bag) (**boys'** bedroom)
F. **Indefinites:** **some, few, many, several, no, any** (and other words)

🙚🙚🙚🙚🙚🙚🙚🙚🙚🙚🙚🙚🙚🙚🙚🙚🙚🙚

Directions: Draw a dotted line under any determiner. Write the determiner
          and the noun that the determiner modifies (goes over to) in the blank.

          Example: Have you lost your backpack?   ___your **backpack**___

1. Ms. Jones, our music teacher, just arrived.   _____

2. Please put this check into my bag.   _____

                                                      _____

3. Several huge owls flew from that tree.   _____

                                                      _____

4. Has their favorite game been played?   _____

5. She hit the cymbal with a padded drumstick.   _____

                                                      _____

6. Peter's friend owns many horses.   _____

                                                      _____

7. No reason had been given for his behavior.   _____

                                                      _____

8. These muffins are too dry.   _____

Determiners are yellow lights. When you approach one, slow down and check it carefully. It will help you to identify many nouns.

However, not all nouns have determiners.

<u>Remember that a noun names a person, place, thing, or idea.</u>

Example: Mom asked our neighbor a question about quilts.

Mom asked *our* **neighbor** *a* **question** about **quilts**.

Note that there are no determiners in front of the nouns, <u>Mom</u> or <u>quilts</u>. Determiners definitely help you to identify nouns. *However*, you will need to think about what nouns are when identifying them.

🙠🙠🙠🙠🙠🙠🙠🙠🙠🙠🙠🙠🙠

Directions: Circle any noun. (You may wish to place a wavy line under each determiner as a guide to identifying nouns.)

1. One puppy wagged its little, curly tail.

2. A police car pulled onto the highway from an exit.

3. Dad bought three pears, two ripe bananas, and several plums.

4. During their trip to Chicago, Mark and his sister visited many museums.

5. Put Jan's stroller, playpen, and bag in that large closet.

6. Your idea made money for our fundraiser last winter.

7. Yesterday, some men met to discuss several important topics.

8. No swans ever glide on this pond in the city's park.

9. Did you meet Leah's parents at her wedding in June?

10. Three computer experts are studying this virus problem.

Name_____   **NOUNS**

Date_____ _15_____   **Possessives**

Singular means one.

> one boy

Possessive means to possess or to own.

> a jacket belonging to a boy

To form the possessive of any singular noun, add *'s*.

> boy*'s* jacket

This form is called the singular possessive. It is a singular noun showing ownership.

Add *'s* even if the word ends in *s*.   Example: Chris*'s* jacket

ৰৡৰৡৰৡৰৡৰৡৰৡৰৡৰৡৰৡৰৡৰৡৰৡৰৡ

Directions: Write the possessive of each singular noun and the item(s) owned.

1. a toy belonging to a baby - _____

2. magazines belonging to her sister - _____

3. a belt belonging to Jasmin - _____

4. a stall for a horse - _____

5. parties given for an ambassador - _____

6. many clients of a hairstylist - _____

7. the shape of an iris - _____

8. doors on our cupboard - _____

9. a handle on a coffeepot - _____

10. mail belonging to Mr. Paas - _____

11. jewelry owned by that woman - _____

104

NOUNS

Possessives

Plural means more than one.

two boys   several boys

Possessive means to possess or to own.

a tree house belonging to two boys

To form the possessive of any plural noun that ends in *s*, add '.

boys' tree house

To form the possessive of any plural noun that does NOT

end in *s*, add '*s*.   children's theater

This form is called the plural possessive. It is a plural noun showing ownership.

ৰ্চৰ্চৰ্চৰ্চৰ্চৰ্চৰ্চৰ্চৰ্চৰ্চৰ্চৰ্চৰ্চৰ্চৰ্চৰ্চৰ্চৰ্চৰ্চ

Directions: Write the plural noun. Then, write the plural possessive and the item(s) owned.

1.   tadpole - _____

      a creek shared by more than one tadpole - _____

2.   salesman - _____

      a meeting for more than one salesman - _____

3.   dancer - _____

      a teacher belonging to more than one dancer - _____

4.   piglet - _____

      a pen where more than one piglet lives - _____

5.   policeman - _____

      an office occupied by more than one policeman - _____

105

Singular means one.   one chipmunk

Plural means more than one.   three chipmunks

Possessive means to possess or to own.

1. **To form the possessive of any singular noun, add '*s*.**

    bird'*s* beak

2. **To form the possessive of any plural noun that ends in *s*, add '.**

    birds' nest (a nest belonging to more than one bird)

3. **To form the possessive of any plural noun that does NOT end in *s*, add '*s*.**

    octopus

    octopi's behavior (the behavior of more than one octopus)

ﳰﳰﳰﳰﳰﳰﳰﳰﳰﳰﳰﳰﳰﳰﳰﳰﳰﳰﳰﳰ

Directions: Write the possessive form and the item(s) owned in each blank.

1. a bone belonging to one dog - _____

    a bone belonging to more than one dog - _____

2. a patient attended by one nurse - _____

    a patient attended by more than one nurse - _____

3. a boat owned by a woman - _____

    a boat owned by more than one woman - _____

4. a campsite used by one family - _____

    a campsite used by more than one family - _____

5. hamsters belonging to a child - _____

    hamsters belonging to more than one child - _____

Possessive means to possess or to own.

1. **To form the possessive of any singular noun, add 's.**

    bracelet**'s** clasp

2. **To form the possessive of any plural noun that ends in s, add '.**

    doctors' conference

3. **To form the possessive of any plural noun that does NOT end in s, add 's.**

    ox

    oxen's barn (a barn belonging to more than one ox)

Directions: Write the possessive form and the item(s) owned in each blank.

1. drawings created by one artist - _____

    an exhibit shared by more than one artist - _____

2. a display done by a florist - _____

    an expo attended by more than one florist - _____

3. plans made by one councilwoman - _____

    plans made by more than one councilwoman - _____

4. a deal signed by Mr. Nicks - _____

    a deal signed by two brothers - _____

5. a hiking trail cleared by a city - _____

    a hiking trail cleared by more than one city - _____

6. shows done by one producer - _____

    shows done by more than one producer - _____

Possessive means to possess or to own.

1. **To form the possessive of any singular noun, add 's.**

   kite's string

2. **To form the possessive of any plural noun that ends in s, add '.**

   toddlers' exercise class

3. **To form the possessive of any plural noun that does NOT end in s, add 's.**

   goose

   geese's noise

Directions: Write the possessive form and the item(s) owned in each blank.

1. pastries created by a chef - _____

2. a boxcar owned by Rex - _____

3. tools shared by more than one craftsman - _____

4. baseballs signed by several athletes - _____

5. a bullpen for one team - _____

6. margins on a paper - _____

7. toe rings owned by my aunt - _____

8. an apartment shared by two boys - _____

9. a shawl knitted by Grandma - _____

10. bushes purchased by several gardeners - _____

11. the tip of an iceberg - _____

12. necklaces designed by Gus - _____

To form the possessive of any singular noun, add 's.
To form the possessive of any plural noun that ends in s, add '.
To form the possessive of any plural noun that does NOT end in s, add 's.

చేఱచేఱచేఱచేఱచేఱచేఱచేఱచేఱచేఱచేఱచేఱచేఱచేఱచేఱ

Directions: Circle the correct possessive form:

1.   marbles owned by Sam: Sam's marbles   Sams' marbles

2.   drums owned by two boys: boy's drums   boys' drums

3.   an apartment shared by two girls: girls' apartment   girl's apartment

4.   a magnet belonging to Janice: Janice's magnet   Janices' magnet

5.   a picnic shared by two families: family's picnic   families' picnic

6.   cap on a radiator: radiators' cap   radiator's cap

7.   the schedules of several pilots: pilots' schedules   pilot's schedules

8.   pictures drawn by Les: Les's pictures   Les pictures

9.   cookies baked by Marco: Marco's cookies   Marcos' cookies

10. soup made by more than one man: men's soup   mens' soup

11. an office shared by two doctors: doctor's office   doctors' office

12. menus created by a cook: cooks' menus   cook's menus

13. a road used by two ranches: ranches' road   ranch's road

14. a stamp on a card: cards' stamp   card's stamp

15. damage caused by two storms   storm's damage   storms' damage

16. sketches by more than one artist: artists' sketches   artist's sketches

109

Name_____   **NOUNS**

Date_____22_____   **Direct Objects/Indirect Objects**

Review:

A noun may serve as a **subject** of a sentence.

Example: **Ginny** bought her husband a tractor for their farm.

A noun may serve as a **direct object** of a sentence.

                                       D.O.

Example: Ginny bought her husband a **tractor** for their farm. (the object she bought)

A noun may serve as an **object of a preposition**.

                                            O.P.

Example: Ginny bought her husband a tractor for their **farm**.

                                    (*for their farm* = prepositional phrase)

New:

A noun may serve as an **indirect object**. **An indirect object is the receiver of** *some* **direct objects.**

                Example: A dentist gave his patient a new toothbrush.

                                                  D.O.

Find the parts of the example: A <u>dentist</u> <u>gave</u> his patient a new toothbrush.

You can mentally insert *to* or *for* **before** an indirect object.

                           to   **I.O.**   **D.O.**

              A <u>dentist</u> <u>gave</u> **/** his patient a new toothbrush.

Look at our original example.

                         for   **I.O.**   **D.O.**

          <u>Ginny</u> <u>bought</u> **/** her husband a tractor for their farm.

When a sentence has a direct object, check to see if it also contains an indirect object.

<u>Remember: You can mentally place **to** or **for** before an indirect object.</u>

        🐛🐛🐛🐛🐛🐛🐛🐛🐛🐛🐛🐛🐛🐛🐛🐛🐛🐛🐛🐛

Directions: Underline the subject once and the verb twice. Label the direct object- **D.O.** Write a noun that will serve as an indirect object in the blank.

           to

1. Mom handed **/** _____ a rake.

              for

2. Grandpa baked **/** his _____ a special dinner.

           to

3. Parker gave **/** her _____ sugarless gum.

               for

4. A nail technician ordered **/** a _____ some hand cream.

110

A noun may serve as an **indirect object**. **An indirect object is the receiver of** *some* **direct objects.**

You can mentally insert **to** or **for before** an indirect object.

                             to   **I.O.**   **D.O.**
        A <u>painter</u> <u>sent</u> **/** the owner a bill.

                             for   **I.O.**   **D.O.**
        The <u>man</u> <u>fixed</u> / his date a nice dinner.

<u>When a sentence has a direct object, check to see if it also contains an indirect object.</u>

<u>Remember: You can mentally place **to** or **for** before an indirect object.</u>

        ھ ھ ھ ھ ھ ھ ھ ھ ھ ھ ھ ھ ھ ھ ھ ھ ھ ھ ھ

Directions: Write **to** or **for** above the **/**. Circle the indirect object.

1.   A guide told / the group the history of the old mansion.

2.   The child drew / his parents a picture of their family.

3.   Several gallery owners sent / art buyers cards concerning a show.

4.   Kammi fixed / the children grilled-cheese sandwiches.

5.   The teacher asked / several students the same question.

6.   Nan printed / her daughter a note.

7.   Mom bought / her co-worker lunch today.

8.   One French poodle gave / her master a lick on his hand.

9.   The landlord makes / new owners a few extra keys.

10.   Dina presented / the bride and groom a wedding gift.

11.   A banker copied / the couple three pages of the house contract.

12.   Has Mrs. Brau sent / her godmother an invitation to the ball?

Name_____   **NOUNS**

Date_____24_____ **Direct Objects/Indirect Objects**

A noun may serve as an **indirect object**. An indirect object is the receiver of *some* direct objects.

You can mentally insert **to** or **for before** an indirect object.

for   **I.O.**   **D.O.**

Those <u>seamstresses</u> <u>make</u> / children little beanbags.

to   **I.O.**   **D.O.**

That <u>teacher</u> <u>mailed</u> / her students cards.

When a sentence has a direct object, check to see if it also contains an indirect object.
Remember: You can mentally place **to** or **for** before an indirect object.

Directions: Cross out any prepositional phrases. Underline the subject once and the verb or verb phrase twice. Label the direct object - **D.O.** Label the indirect object - **I.O.**

1.   A guide told the group the history of the old mansion.

2.   The child drew his parents a picture.

3.   Several gallery owners sent art buyers cards concerning a show.

4.   Kammi fixed the children grilled-cheese sandwiches.

5.   The teacher asked several students the same question.

6.   Nan printed her daughter a note.

7.   Mom bought her co-worker lunch today.

8.   One French poodle gave her master a lick on his hand.

9.   The landlord makes new owners a few extra keys.

10.   Tate presented the bride and groom a wedding gift.

11.   A banker copied the couple three pages of the house contract.

12.   Has Mrs. Brau sent her godmother an invitation to the ball?
112

When a sentence has a direct object, check to see if it also contains an indirect object. Remember: You can mentally place *to* or *for* before an indirect object.

for   **I.O.**   **D.O.**
The <u>chef</u> <u>made</u> / his guests a shrimp salad.

to **I.O.**   **D.O.**
<u>I</u> <u>threw</u> / Jan a football.

డ9డ9డ9డ9డ9డ9డ9డ9డ9డ9డ9డ9డ9డ9డ9

A. Directions: Cross out any prepositional phrases. Underline the subject once and the verb or verb phrase twice. Label the direct object – **D.O.**

1.   The father ordered a scooter.

2.   Marco prepared a spinach dip.

3.   Chessa baked a roast with carrots.

4.   That young woman sends many packages.

5.   Miss Sims sewed two long gowns.

6.   A stockbroker bought a thousand shares of stock.

B. Directions: Cross out any prepositional phrases. Underline the subject once and the verb or verb phrase twice. Label the direct object – **D.O.** Label the indirect object - **I.O.**

1.   The father ordered his children a scooter.

2.   Marco prepared his wife a spinach dip.

3.   Chessa baked her parents a roast with carrots.

4.   The young woman sends the soldier packages.

5.   Miss Sims sewed the mayor's wife two long gowns.

6.   A stockbroker bought Mrs. Hernandez a thousand shares of stock.

113

PREDICATE NOMINATIVES

A noun may serve as a predicate nominative.

Remember: The complete predicate of a sentence usually begins with the verb and goes to the end of a sentence.

My ball **rolled** down a steep hill.
complete predicate

Last fall, her dad **became** a sports announcer.
complete predicate

A predicate nominative occurs after a linking verb.

ཀ ཀ ཀ ཀ ཀ ཀ ཀ ཀ ཀ

Linking Verbs:

to feel	to smell	to grow	to stay
to taste	to seem	to remain	to become
to look	to sound	to appear	to be (is, am, are, was, were, be, being, been)

ཀ ཀ ཀ ཀ ཀ ཀ ཀ ཀ ཀ

A predicate nominative is a noun (or pronoun) that occurs <u>after</u> a linking verb and <u>means the same as the subject</u>.

P.N.
Example: Their <u>neighbor</u> in Alaska <u>was</u> Mr. Hare.

To determine if a sentence contains a predicate nominative, do the following:

1. Find the subject and verb.

   (Delete any prepositional phrases. A predicate nominative will not

   appear in a prepositional phrase.)

   Their <u>neighbor</u> ~~in Alaska~~ <u>was</u> Mr. Hare.

2. Ask yourself if the verb is on the linking verb list.

   Was is on the linking verb list. *Was* **may** serve as a linking verb here.

3. If the verb is on that list, see if there is a noun after the verb that
   means the same as the subject.

   <u>neighbor</u>　　　　=　　　Mr. Hare

4. Try inverting the sentence to prove a predicate nominative.

   P.N.
   Their <u>neighbor</u> <u>is</u> Mr. Hare.

   Inverted form:　　*Mr. Hare is their neighbor.*

A noun may serve as a predicate nominative. A predicate nominative occurs <u>after</u> a linking verb *<u>and means the same as the subject</u>*.

To determine if a sentence contains a predicate nominative, do the following:
1.   Delete any prepositional phrases. Find the subject and verb.

The <u>winner</u> <s>of the contest</s> <u>is</u> my collie.

2.   Ask yourself if the verb is on the linking verb list.   **Yes!** *<u>Is</u>!*
3.   Is there a noun after the verb that means the same as the subject?

<u>winner</u>   =   collie

4.   Invert the sentence to prove a predicate nominative.

P.N.

The <u>winner</u> <s>of the contest</s> <u>is</u> my collie.

Inverted form: My collie is the winner (of the contest).

ༀༀༀༀༀༀༀༀༀༀༀༀༀༀༀༀༀༀༀༀ

Directions: Cross out any prepositional phrases. Underline the subject once and the verb twice. Label a predicate nominative – **P.N.** Then, write the inverted form of the sentence in the blank.

1.   Miss Shell is our teacher.   _____

2.   My favorite fruit is a pear.   _____

3.   The girl in pigtails is my sister.   _____

4.   Their father was the mayor of Ajo.   _____

5.   Your best choice is honesty.   _____

6.   Jacob will be your server.   _____

7.   Our black and white cat is Oreo.   _____

was

8.   Lani has become the best plumber.   _____

116

A **predicate nominative** occurs <u>after</u> a linking verb and means the same as the subject.

Remember:
   To determine if a sentence contains a predicate nominative, do the following:
   1. Delete any prepositional phrases. Find the subject and verb.

   A <u>pansy</u> <u>is</u> a small flower ~~with tiny leaves.~~

   2. Ask yourself if the verb is on the linking verb list.   Yes! *<u>Is</u>!*
   3. Is there a noun after the verb that means the same as the subject?

                                             P. N.
                     <u>**pansy**</u>   **=**   **flower**

   4. Invert the sentence to prove a predicate nominative.

         Inverted form: A small flower with tiny leaves is a pansy.
         ૐ ૐ ૐ ૐ ૐ ૐ ૐ ૐ ૐ ૐ ૐ ૐ ૐ ૐ ૐ ૐ ૐ ૐ ૐ

Directions: Cross out any prepositional phrases. Underline the subject once
              and the verb twice. Label a predicate nominative – **P.N.** Then,
              write the inverted form of the sentence in the blank.

1. His mother is my piano teacher.

   _____

2. The person behind the desk is Mrs. Dell.

   _____

3. The first bronco rider was Cammi's uncle.

   _____

4. Our goal for the fundraiser is new playground equipment.

   _____

             was
5. Tate remained the wrestling champion for three years.

   _____

A **predicate nominative** occurs <u>after</u> a linking verb and means the same as the subject.

🙐🙐🙐🙐🙐🙐🙐🙐🙐🙐🙐🙐🙐🙐🙐🙐🙐🙐

Directions: Cross out any prepositional phrases. Underline the subject once and the verb twice. Label a predicate nominative – **P.N.** Then, write the inverted form of the sentence in the blank.

1. The new coaches were our former history teachers.

   _____

2. A platypus is a mammal with webbed feet.

   _____

3. The scum on their pool is algae.

   _____

4. Juan's mother is the owner of that Mexican food restaurant.

   _____

5. A toddler became the youngest reader in the library's reading program.

   _____

6. The bride's last name remained Stellar.

   _____

7. The winner in the javelin throw at the first track meet was Parker.

   _____

8. Her reward from the company was a bonus.

   _____

A. **Concrete and Abstract Nouns:**

Directions: Write **C** in the blank if the noun is concrete and **A** if it is abstract.

1. _____	potato		6. _____	train
2. _____	factory		7. _____	courage
3. _____	love		8. _____	freedom
4. _____	bumper		9. _____	skunk
5. _____	silliness		10. _____	fear

ରେ ରେ ରେ ରେ ରେ ରେ ରେ ରେ ରେ ରେ ରେ ରେ

B. **Common and Proper Nouns:**

Directions: Place a ◆ if the noun is common.

1. ___	ANNA	5. ___	STAR	9. ___	CANADA
2. ___	BANK	6. ___	ALABAMA	10. ___	ANIMAL
3. ___	BOTTLE	7. ___	CARPENTER	11. ___	CANAL
4. ___	ASIA	8. ___	FORT	12. ___	KANGAROO

ରେ ରେ ରେ ରେ ରେ ରେ ରେ ରେ ରେ ରେ ରେ ରେ

C. **Noun or Adjective:**

Remember: The same word may serve as a noun in one sentence and as an adjective (describing word) in another sentence.

Examples: A. I saw a **fish** in a pond.   *Fish* is a noun in this sentence.

B. I ate a **fish** sandwich.   _fish sandwich_

Fish is an adjective in this sentence because it describes sandwich.

Directions: On the short line provided, write **N** if the boldfaced word serves as a noun and **A** if the word serves as an adjective (describing word). If the word is an adjective, write the word and the noun it modifies.

1. _____   A farmer planted **corn** in a field.   _____

2. _____   Do you like **corn** chowder?   _____

3. _____   **Silk** ties are on sale at that shop.   _____

4. _____   **Silk** is a very soft fabric.   _____

ॐॐॐॐॐॐॐॐॐॐॐ

D. **Singular and Plural Nouns:**
   Directions: Circle the correct spelling of each plural noun.
   Use a dictionary if necessary.

1. mysteries	mysterys	9. belts	beltes
2. torchs	torches	10. taxes	taxs
3. pullies	pulleys	11. whiffs	whives
4. womans	women	12. informations	information
5. tomatos	tomatoes	13. moths	mothes
6. deer	deers	14. troopes	troops
7. calfs	calves	15. replys	replies
8. lips	lipses	16. lens	lenses

ॐॐॐॐॐॐॐॐॐॐॐ

E. **Determiners:**
   Directions: Place a ✓ in the blank if the boldfaced word is a determiner. If
   the word serves as a determiner, write the boldfaced word and
   the noun that it modifies (goes over to) in the wide blank.

1. ___   May I please have **two** without frosting? _____

2. ___   You must order **two** items to get one free. _____

3. ___   Do you have **this** in a larger size? _____

120

4. __ Are you fine with **this** decision? _____

5. __ **Some** business cards have been printed. _____

6. __ **Some** were excused early. _____

ক্ষ ক্ষ ক্ষ ক্ষ ক্ষ ক্ষ ক্ষ ক্ষ ক্ষ ক্ষ ক্ষ ক্ষ

F. **Possessive Nouns:**
   Directions: Write the possessive form and the item(s) owned in each blank.

1. pictures belonging to Maddy - _____

2. a home owned by her brother - _____

3. a lease signed by two brothers - _____

4. pamphlets belonging to a travel agent - _____

5. a meeting attended by more than one woman - _____

ক্ষ ক্ষ ক্ষ ক্ষ ক্ষ ক্ষ ক্ষ ক্ষ ক্ষ ক্ষ ক্ষ ক্ষ

G. **Nouns Used as Subject, Direct Object, and Indirect Object:**
   Directions: Write **S.** if the noun serves as a subject.
                 Write **D.O.** if the noun serves as a direct object.
                 Write **I.O.** if the noun serves as an indirect object.

1. _____ Does an addax drink **water**?

2. _____ Todd ordered his **family** a grill.

3. _____ His black-and-white-striped **flashlight** is too dim.

4. _____ A teacher read the **students** a story.

5. _____ Mom placed **candles** on my cake.

H. **Predicate Nominatives:**

Directions: Cross out any prepositional phrases. Underline the subject once and the verb twice. Label a predicate nominative – **P.N.** Then, write the inverted form of the sentence in the blank.

Remember: **A predicate nominative occurs <u>after</u> a linking verb and means the same as the subject.**

1. Their residence is a new apartment on Potter Avenue.

_____

2. Those men were the winners of the logging contest.

_____

3. The first settlers in Kentucky were pioneers with Daniel Boone.

_____

4. That old barn is the oldest building in this village.

_____

☙☙☙☙☙☙☙☙☙☙☙

I. **Identifying Nouns:**

Directions: Circle any nouns.

Remember: **Determiners will help you to find some nouns. You may want to box them in order to help you.**

1. Three golden butterflies with many orange dots on its wings flew by.

2. Nan's daughter has planted a tree and several rose bushes in her yard.

3. Will you use that paisley tie on a striped shirt with your new suit?

4. Twelve charms hung on an unusual bracelet without any clasp.

5. On Mondays, those joggers wind through the park before dawn.

Name_____

Date_____

A. List of Prepositions:

Directions: Write the prepositions.

1. abo_____	20. b_____	39. pa_____
2. abo_____	21. con_____	40. reg_____
3. acr_____	22. do_____	41. si_____
4. aft_____	23. dur_____	42. th_____
5. aga_____	24. ex_____	43. thr_____
6. alo_____	25. fo_____	44. t_____
7. ami_____	26. fr_____	45. tow_____
8. amo_____	27. i_____	46. un_____
9. aro_____	28. ins_____	47. und_____
10. a_____	29. int_____	48. unt_____
11. ato_____	30. li_____	49. u_____
12. bef_____	31. ne_____	50. upo_____
13. beh_____	32. o_____	51. wi_____
14. bel_____	33. o_____	52. wi_____
15. ben_____	34. o_____	53. wi_____
16. bes_____	35. o_____	
17. bet_____	36. o_____	
18. bey_____	37. ou_____	
19. bu_____	38. ov_____	

B. **Subject/Verb:**
    Directions: Cross out any prepositional phrases. Underline the subject once
                     and the verb twice.

1. Monkeys jumped through the branches.

2. The travelers drove for three hours without a break.

3. Kammie sweeps beneath her bed after dusting.

శ్రీశ్రీశ్రీశ్రీశ్రీశ్రీశ్రీశ్రీశ్రీశ్రీ

C. **Compound Objects of the Preposition:**
    Directions: Cross out any prepositional phrases. Underline the subject once
                     and the verb twice. Label the object of the preposition – **O.P.**

1. Dakota wrote a report concerning hurricanes and tornados.

2. Our coach sat between Darla and me.

3. This large envelope is for Tommy or his grandpa.

శ్రీశ్రీశ్రీశ్రీశ్రీశ్రీశ్రీశ్రీశ్రీశ్రీ

D. **Compound Subjects:**
    Directions: Cross out any prepositional phrases. Underline the subject once
                     and the verb or verb phrase twice.

1. Our phonebook and pens are in the first drawer beside the sink.

2. During spring break, Tessa and her mother drove to Ohio.

3. The host of the television show or his guests will judge the event.

శ్రీశ్రీశ్రీశ్రీశ్రీశ్రీశ్రీశ్రీశ్రీశ్రీ

E. **Imperative Sentences:**
    Directions: Cross out any prepositional phrases. Underline the subject once
                     and the verb twice.

1. Press your hand against this board.

2. Clean your fingernails with this nailbrush.

124

F. **Infinitives:**
   Directions: Cross out any prepositional phrases. Place parentheses **( )** around any infinitive. Underline the subject once and the verb twice.

1. The children want to go to a water park.

2. She plans to leave before breakfast.

3. I need to learn about koalas and panda bears.

☙☙☙☙☙☙☙☙☙☙☙☙

G. **Preposition or Adverb?:**
   Directions: Cross out any prepositional phrases. Underline the subject once and the verb twice. Write **A** if the boldfaced word is an adverb. Write **P** if the boldfaced word is a preposition that begins a prepositional phrase.

1. _____   Our guest came **inside**.

2. _____   His horse is **inside** the barn.

3. _____   One tree trimmer crawled **out** onto a branch.

4. _____   Several wasps flew **out** the window.

☙☙☙☙☙☙☙☙☙☙☙☙

H. **Verb Phrases and *Not*:**
   Directions: Cross out any prepositional phrases. Box *not* or *n't*.
                Underline the subject once and the verb or verb phrase twice.

1. You are not in this picture with your relatives.

2. Our telephone hadn't rung all afternoon.

3. She may not have been at an art show.

4. That tractor-trailer driver has not driven to Buffalo.

I. **The Verb, *To Be*:**
    Directions: Fill in the blank with the correct form of the infinitive, *to be*.

1. Last week, Sam _____ in Idaho on a fishing trip.

2. Presently, I _____ here.

3. The other day, we _____ near a beach.

4. Tomorrow, Marco _____ in Spain.

ᔐᔐᔐᔐᔐᔐᔐᔐᔐᔐᔐᔐ

J. **Contractions:**
    Directions: Write the contraction.

1. are not - _____   6. we are - _____

2. does not - _____   7. who is - _____

3. what is - _____   8 . cannot - _____

4. they are - _____   9. should not - _____

5. must not - _____   10. I shall - _____

ᔐᔐᔐᔐᔐᔐᔐᔐᔐᔐᔐᔐ

K. **You're/Your, It's/Its, and They're/Their/There:**
    Directions: Circle the correct word.

1. I think (it's, its) too early for a snack.

2. (You're, Your) in a very happy mood today.

3. Van went (they're, their, there) looking for you.

4. (They're, Their, There) going to the hospital to visit (they're, their, there) uncle.

5. (It's, Its) so hot that (you're, your) bananas are overly ripe.

126

L. **Auxiliary (Helping) Verbs:**

      Directions: Write the 23 helping verbs.

1. d_____   7. m_____   13. c_____   19. w_____

2. d_____   8. m_____   14. s_____   20. w_____

3. d_____   9. m_____   15. w_____   21. b_____

4. h_____   10. c_____   16. i_____   22. b_____

5. h_____   11. s_____   17. a_____   23. b_____

6. h_____   12. w_____   18. a_____

ൟൟൟൟൟൟൟൟൟൟൟൟ

M. **Verb Phrases:**

      Directions: Cross out any prepositional phrases. Underline the subject once and the verb phrase twice.

1. One rider has washed his bicycle after the race.

2. You should have stopped for gas.

3. Does your mother cook hamburgers on her new grill?

ൟൟൟൟൟൟൟൟൟൟൟൟ

N. **Compound Verbs:**

      Directions: Cross out any prepositional phrases. Underline the subject once and the verb or verb phrase twice.

1. One cow in the herd lifted its head and mooed.

2. Carlo bought a truck and sold his car to his brother.

3. That handyman paints, tiles, and installs lights without a helper.

4. Have you heard or seen any news about an earthquake?

5. A dessert chef melted chocolate bits in a pan and whipped sugar into it.

O. **Irregular Verbs:**
    Directions: Underline the subject once and the correct verb phrase twice.

1. I have (ran, run) there.

2. He may have (fell, fallen).

3. Our bell must have (rang, rung).

4. This swing is (broke, broken).

5. Have you (taken, took) a mint?

6. Lou should have (swum, swam) longer.

7. Jo had (did, done) his homework.

8. Has he ever (ate, eaten) clams?

9. Josh might have (flew, flown) alone.

10. We could have (went, gone) with him.

11. Medical kits had been (chosen, chose).

ﺶﻫﻮﺶﻫﻮﺶﻫﻮﺶﻫﻮﺶﻫﻮﺶﻫﻮﺶﻫﻮﺶﻫﻮﺶﻫﻮﺶﻫﻮﺶﻫﻮ

P. **Subjects, Verbs, and Direct Objects:**
    Directions: Cross out any prepositional phrases. Underline the subject once
                    and the verb/verb phrase twice. Label any direct object – **D.O.**

1. She taped her papers together.

2. Have you cleaned the spots on your shoes?

3. Before the basketball game, the players threw the ball to each other.

4. Throughout the winter, workers drove snow plows during blizzards.

5. One of the lions lifted its head and roared loudly.

Q. **Sit/Set, Lie/Lay, and Rise/Raise:**
    Directions: Delete any prepositional phrases. Underline the subject once
                 and the verb/verb phrase twice. Label any direct object – **D.O.**

1. The best man at the wedding (rose, raised) his glass for a toast.

2. She (lay, laid) on the bench with large orange cushions.

3. Ron (set, sat) his cooler outside his back door.

4. Your skateboard is (lying, laying) on its side.

5. Were you (setting, sitting) on the bleachers before the baseball game?

6. I have (lain, laid) the fabric softener on the washing machine.

7. Smoke is (rising, raising) from our small campfire.

ﻌﻌﻌﻌﻌﻌﻌﻌﻌﻌﻌ

R. **Tenses:**
    Directions: Underline the subject once and the verb or verb phrase
                  twice. Write the tense (*present*, *past*, or *future*) in the blank.

1. _____ We bought fresh vegetables.

2. _____ My foot aches.

3. _____ Will you finish later?

4. _____ Tally dreams often.

5. _____ A black Labrador rescued his owner.

6. _____ I shall give you my cell phone.

7. _____ These cups are silver.

8. _____ Large magnolia trees grow nearby.

S. Linking Verbs:
   Directions: Write the linking verbs.

1. to _____   6. to _____   11. to_____   d. _____

2. to _____   7. to _____   12. to _____   e. _____

3. to _____   8. to _____   a. _____   f. _____

4. to _____   9. to _____   b. _____   g. _____

5. to _____   10. to _____   c. _____   h. _____

&&&&&&&&&&&&&&&

T. Action Verb or Linking Verb?:

   Directions: Write **A** if the verb is action; write **L** if the verb is linking.

1. _____   He **appears** calm.

2. _____   His watch **stopped**.

3. _____   Our goat **bleats**.

4. _____   He **looked** at his map.

5. _____   This apple **tastes** tart.

6. _____   The cat **jumped** onto a table.

&&&&&&&&&&&&&&&

U. Linking Verbs and Predicate Adjectives:
   Directions: Write **L** in the space if the verb is linking. Place a form of *to be*
                  above each verb to help determine if the verb is linking.

   **Remember: Try placing *is, am, are, was,* or *were* in place of the verb. If the meaning of the sentence
   does not change, the verb is probably linking.**

1. _____   She <u>seemed</u> confident.   3. _____   Tabby <u>uses</u> a litter box.

2. _____   My speech <u>sounds</u> slurred.   4. _____   This popcorn <u>tastes</u> salty.

130

V. **Linking Verbs and Predicate Adjectives:**
Directions: Delete any prepositional phrases. Underline the subject once and the verb/verb phrase twice. Label any predicate adjective – **P.A.**

1. That truck with wide mud flaps is new.

2. The child is growing sleepy.

3. His grandfather became excited about their planned rapids trip.

🙠🙠🙠🙠🙠🙠🙠🙠🙠🙠🙠🙠

W. **Subject-Verb Agreement:**
Directions: Delete any prepositional phrases. Underline the subject once.
Underline the verb/verb phrase that agrees with the subject twice.

1. One lizard (hides, hide) under our bushes.

2. These actors (learns, learn) lines easily.

3. Some onions (smell, smells) strong.

4. The top of his hands (have, has) a rash.

5. Their butler (does(n't), do(n't)) answer their phone.

6. Our palm trees (sway, sways) in the wind.

🙠🙠🙠🙠🙠🙠🙠🙠🙠🙠🙠🙠

X. **Transitive and Intransitive Verbs:**
Directions: Underline the subject once and the verb or verb phrase twice.
Label any direct object – **D.O.** Write **T** if the verb is transitive;
write **I** if the verb is intransitive.
Remember: A transitive verb will have a direct object.
D.O.T. > Direct Object = Transitive

1. _____   We solved the mystery.

2. _____   Mom does crossword puzzles.

3. _____   The server handed us menus.

4. _____   Jamilla laughed softly.

Name_____

Date_____

Adjectives describe.

Directions: Write three adjectives that describe each noun.

1.   peach

_____
_____
_____

2.   parrot

_____
_____
_____

3.   bin

_____
_____
_____

4.   chips

_____
_____
_____

5.   park

_____
_____
_____

6.   skateboard

_____
_____
_____

7.   doctor

_____
_____
_____

8.   bottle

_____
_____
_____

9.   eggs

_____
_____
_____

10.   car

_____
_____
_____

Adjectives describe.

Directions: Write a descriptive adjective in each blank. Draw an arrow from the descriptive adjective to the noun it modifies (goes over to). Do not use colors. Try not to reuse any adjectives.

1. A. a _____ hole   B. a _____ hole

2. A. this _____ soup   B. this _____ soup

3. A. the _____ bug   B. the _____ bug

4. A. many _____ tires   B. many _____ tires

5. A. _____ milk   B. _____ milk

6. A. a _____ camera   B. a _____ camera

7. A. those _____ sheets   B. those _____ sheets

8. A. a _____ beard   B. a _____ beard

9. A. her _____ toe   B. her _____ toe

10. A. some _____ boxes   B. some _____ boxes

11. A. your _____ shirt   B. your _____ shirt

Adjectives describe.

Directions: Write a descriptive adjective in each blank. Draw an arrow from the descriptive adjective to the noun it modifies (goes over to).

1.   They traveled down a _____ road.

2.   Ali likes to eat _____ bread for breakfast.

3.   Those floors were scrubbed with _____ water.

4.   Two girls joined a _____ team last week.

5.   _____ sundaes are very tasty.

6.   Miss Dobbs enjoys _____ days.

7.   This book about _____ bears is interesting.

8.   A _____ sound can be annoying.

9.   Our family went on a/an _____ hike.

10. His friend likes _____ books.

11. A teller spoke with a (an) _____ lady for ten minutes.

12. What do you think of _____ music?

LIMITING ADJECTIVES

You have learned that many adjectives describe.

There is another type of adjectives called **limiting** or **determining adjectives**.

The good news is that you just learned these as signals in the noun unit. Therefore, you should be able to find and use them easily. Do you remember these classifications?

Classification of Limiting (Determining) Adjectives:

✡ **Articles:**   **a, an, the**

> Example: I ate **an** orange.

> Note: Any time you see *a, an,* or *the*, mark each as an adjective.
>
> They are also called *articles*.

✡ **Demonstratives:**   **this, that, these, those**

> Example: I met **that** race-car driver.

Use *this* and *that* with <u>singular</u> nouns.   I want this <u>bag</u>.   I want that <u>bag</u>.
Use *these* and *those* with <u>plural</u> nouns.   I want these <u>bags</u>.   I want those <u>bags</u>.

Be careful with demonstratives. If *this, that, these,* or *those* stands alone, it serves as a pronoun.

> Do you want ***these*** shoes?   **(adjective)**
>
> Do you want ***these***?   **(pronoun)**

✡ **Numbers:**

> Example: We each selected **two** costumes.

Be careful with numbers. If a number stands alone, it serves as a pronoun.

> ***Two*** teams were chosen.   **(adjective)**
>
> ***Two*** were chosen.   **(pronoun)**

135

✿**Possessive Pronouns:**   my, his, her, your, its, our, their, whose

Example: **My** vest is leather.

These are sometimes referred to as possessive pronouns used as adjectives.

✿**Possessive Nouns:**

Examples: I like **Grandpa's** homemade cookies.

The **lions'** den is like a cave.

These are sometimes referred to as possessive nouns used as adjectives.

✿**Indefinites:**   any, few, no, many, most, several, some

Example: I want a **few** minutes of your time.

Be careful with indefinites. If an indefinite stands alone, it is a pronoun.

Few floods occur here.   **(adjective)**

I need a **few**.   **(pronoun)**

✿✿✿✿✿✿✿✿✿✿✿✿✿✿✿✿✿✿✿✿✿✿✿

An adjective modifies another word. *Modifies* means to go over to a word. It answers *what.*

Example: **This** wagon is lime green.

This is an adjective. This what? This wagon! *This* is an **adjective** modifying *wagon*.

However, a word that can be an adjective will sometimes appear **alone** in a sentence. When this happens, the word will not be an adjective. It will be a **pronoun**.

Example: **That** is mine.

That what?   You don't know. *That* is a pronoun.

136

Limiting (Determining) Adjectives:

Articles: a, an, the

Demonstratives: this, that, these, those

Numbers: Example: *seven* points

Possessive Pronouns: my, his, her, your, its, our, their, whose

Possessive Nouns: Example: *Jacy's* comb

Indefinites: any, few, no, many, most, several, some

 howo howo howo howo howo howo howo howo howo howo howo

Directions: Write an appropriate limiting adjective from each category.

1. **Article** – May I have _____ penny?

    Demonstratives – May I have _____ penny?

    Numbers – May I have _____ pennies?

    Possessive pronouns – May I have _____ penny?

    Possessive nouns – May I have _____ penny?

    Indefinites – May I have _____ pennies?

howo howo howo

2. **Article** – _____ magazines were thrown away.

    Demonstratives – _____ magazines were thrown away.

    Numbers – _____ magazines were thrown away.

    Possessive pronouns – _____ magazines were thrown away.

    Possessive nouns – _____ magazines were thrown away.

    Indefinites – _____ magazines were thrown away.

Limiting (Determining) Adjectives:

Articles: a, an, the

Demonstratives: this, that, these, those

Numbers: Example: *three* carrots

Possessive Pronouns: my, his, her, your, its, our, their, whose

Possessive Nouns: Examples: *Jemima's* wish   girls' club

Indefinites: any, few, no, many, most, several, some (There are others.)

ೋೋೋೋೋೋೋೋೋೋೋೋೋೋೋೋೋೋೋ

Directions: Write an appropriate limiting adjective from each category. (Do not use a word twice.) Then, draw an arrow to the noun it modifies (goes over to that word).

1.   (Demonstrative) – You should like _____ pictures.

2.   (Possessive pronoun) – That dog is eating _____ lunch.

3.   (Number) – We need _____ nails to finish the job.

4.   (Article) – Do you have _____ compass?

5.   (Indefinite) – I have not seen _____ turtles in this area.

6.   (Possessive noun) – A _____ front paw was hurt.

7.   (Possessive pronoun) – _____ backpack is like mine.

8.   (Indefinite) – I have _____ money with me.

9.   (Demonstrative) – Did Misty write _____ story?

10.   (Possessive noun) – _____ humor amazes me!

11.   (Number) – Mrs. Jolly has _____ nephews.

12.   (Article) – Do you want _____ balloon with blue stripes?

13.   (Possessive pronoun) – The disc jockey played _____ favorite song.

138

Name_____

Date_____

Directions: Write an appropriate limiting adjective. (Do not use a word twice.)
Draw an arrow to the noun it modifies (goes over to that word).

1.   (Possessive pronoun) – Divers checked _____ equipment.

2.   (Indefinite) – _____ index cards were needed.

3.   (Article) – We chose _____ small teddy bear as a gift.

4.   (Demonstrative) –   Do you want _____ healthy snacks?

5.   (Number) – They earned _____ dollars by mowing yards.

6.   (Possessive noun) – _____ lips are chapped.

7.   (Article) – Kim needs _____ new winter jacket.

8.   (Indefinite) – The party planner bought _____ favors.

9.   (Possessive pronoun) – _____ sunglasses are on the floor.

10.   (Demonstrative) – Please send _____ fax to your company.

11.   (Number) – Tate ordered _____ racing posters.

12.   (Possessive noun) – Have you seen a _____ nest?

13.   (Possessive pronoun) – I like _____ attitude.

14.   (Indefinite) – His agent makes _____ decisions.

15.   (Article) – _____ eagle flew nearby.

16.   (Demonstrative) – May I have _____ tiny tangerine?

17.   (Possessive pronoun) – _____ wand is this?

18.   (Possessive noun) – Yikes! I lost my _____ car keys!

Name_____

Date_____

Remember: **Some words can be limiting adjectives if they modify a noun or pronoun. That same word will not be a limiting adjective if it stands alone.**

Examples: Please turn on *that* fan.   Adjective – *that* fan

May I have *that?*   That what? We don't know.
That is not an adjective.

∞∞∞∞∞∞∞∞∞∞∞∞∞∞∞∞∞∞∞

Directions: Write **Adj.** in the short blank if the boldfaced word serves as a limiting adjective. Write the boldfaced word and the noun it modifies in the blank after the sentence. Write **No** if the boldfaced word does not serve as a limiting adjective.

1. _____   I asked **some** friends to help me.   _____

2. _____   **Some** laughed at the child's remark.   _____

3. _____   **Her** exercise class is fun.   _____

4. _____   Will you go with **her**?   _____

5. _____   Please take **these** with you.   _____

6. _____   Everyone is amused by **these** gerbils.   _____

7. _____   The store had **several** mops on sale.   _____

8. _____   I need **several** for the conference.   _____

9. _____   Were **four** bags of nuts purchased?   _____

10. _____   **Four** of the senators voted against
the bill.

_____

11. _____   I don't know **whose** purse is lost.   _____

12. _____   Do you know **whose** was chosen?   _____

Name_____

Date_____

A. Directions: Circle any limiting adjectives.

1. Four teenagers ordered a pizza with no cheese.

2. That priest visited several families in his parish.

3. Mom's friend sent some seeds for her garden.

4. An engineer presented the twelve awards.

5. We like those chairs without any padding.

&&&&&&&&&&&&&&&&

B. Directions: Circle any descriptive adjectives.

1. Stamp boxes with green swirls have been found.

2. Purple glass cups with curved handles were sold.

3. I want soft, pleated drapes for the bedroom windows.

4. Elephants have huge grey ears and long trunks.

5. Wedding gifts are often wrapped in silver paper with large white bows.

&&&&&&&&&&&&&&&&

C. Directions: Circle limiting <u>and</u> descriptive adjectives.

1. Many good cooks use that old cookbook for special recipes.

2. A knitted, wool sweater with an orange border was her birthday gift.

3. Has Penny's horse been given fresh water and several crisp carrots?

4. My two cousins bought grape juice from our school's snack bar.

5. This satin dress with black polka dots won the designer award.

Proper adjectives are descriptive words derived from proper nouns. Let's review common and proper nouns.

Common Noun	Proper Noun	
country	**E**ngland	(name of a specific country)
city	**T**ampa	(name of a specific city)
continent	**A**sia	(name of a specific continent)

A proper adjective is a descriptive word. It is based on a proper noun and is **capitalized**.

Proper Noun	Proper Adjective	
England	**E**nglish	**E**nglish tea
Tampa	**T**ampa	a **T**ampa park
Asia	**A**sian	an **A**sian landscape

Note that *Tampa* does not change when becoming a proper adjective. Some words do not change.

෨෨෨෨෨෨෨෨෨෨෨෨෨෨෨෨෨෨෨෨෨

Directions: Write the proper adjective for each proper noun. Then, write a word that it might modify on the line next to it.

Example: France - _____**French**_____ _____**bread**_____

1. Italy - _____ _____

2. Africa - _____ _____

3. Mexico - _____ _____

4. America - _____ _____

5. Newport Beach - _____ _____

6. Sweden - _____ _____

7. Clover Club - _____ _____

Name_____

Date_____

Proper adjectives are descriptive words derived from proper nouns.

Common Noun	*Proper Noun*	
town	**K**ingsdale	(name of a specific town)
state	**A**laska	(name of a specific state)
sea	**B**altic **S**ea	(name of a specific sea)

A proper adjective is a descriptive word based on a proper noun. A proper adjective is **capitalized**.

Proper Noun	*Proper Adjective*	
Kingsdale	**K**ingsdale	a **K**ingsdale carnival
Alaska	**A**laskan	an **A**laskan fishing boat
Baltic **S**ea	**B**altic **S**ea	a **B**altic **S**ea storm

Directions: Circle any proper adjective. Draw an arrow to the word it modifies.

1.   Her Hawaiian shirt is very bright.

2.   A French cottage is located on a coastal island.

3.   The Italian singer performed at Sims Hall.

4.   A Washington lawyer opened a new office.

5.   Do you want to go on an African safari?

6.   We attended a United Nations meeting.

7.   Have you seen the Long Beach pier?

8.   His friends visit a Bahamas beach.

9.   A North American airline opened a new Canadian office.

10.   I collect Kennedy coins and Victorian china.

A complete predicate is the part of a sentence that includes the verb and usually the remainder of a sentence.

> Example: Parachutes **opened in the air**.
> *complete predicate*

If a sentence is a **question**, make it into a statement before naming the complete predicate.

> Example: Did you speak with that security guard?
>
> You **did speak with that security guard**.
> *complete predicate*

෴෴෴෴෴෴෴෴෴෴෴෴෴෴෴෴෴෴෴෴

Directions: Place a dotted line under the complete predicate.

1.   An excited puppy scooted across the kitchen floor.

2.   They called the company concerning their loan.

3.   One kayaker lifted his oar over his head.

4.   The drummer laid his sticks on the floor by his stool.

5.   The students write their goals in a notebook.

6.   My grandparents attended a musical at a local theater.

7.   Some of our glue sticks are dry.

8.   Does Pat love to walk in the rain?

9.   Mrs. Reno and her son brought several cakes to the picnic.

10.   Will a shoemaker repair your boot?

11.   Tate's mother and father remained silent about their decision.

12.   Has she placed your contact number in her phone?

A complete predicate is the part of a sentence that includes the verb and usually the remainder of a sentence.

> Example: Her hair is brown with blonde streaks.
> *complete predicate*

~~~~~~

A.   Directions: Place a dotted line under the complete predicate.

1. Sara becomes concerned during storms.

2. This shovel has a broken handle.

3. My toes are sore and muddy.

4. Your hair seems tangled.

~~~~~~

Sometimes, an adjective occurs in the predicate (after a verb) and describes the subject. This is called a predicate adjective.

> P.A.
> Example: This ring is shiny.   ___*shiny* ring___

B.   Directions: Write an adjective in the first blank. Write the same adjective in the sentence below it. Label it **P.A.** - predicate adjective. Then, place a dotted line under the complete predicate.

1. a (an) _____ cat

   The cat is _____.

2. the _____ boys

   The boys are _____.

3. a (an) _____ day

   The day remained _____.

4. a (an) _____ greeting

   Their greeting was _____.

A complete predicate is the part of a sentence that includes the verb and usually the remainder of a sentence.

Example: A herd of buffalo is roaming in a meadow.
complete predicate

Sometimes an adjective occurs after the verb but describes the subject. This is called a predicate adjective.

🙢🙢🙢🙢🙢🙢🙢🙢🙢🙢🙢🙢🙢🙢🙢🙢

Directions: Write an adjective in the blank provided. Then, underline the complete predicate with a dotted line. Label the predicate adjective — **P.A.**

1. Our hot dogs tasted _____.

2. These plums are _____.

3. You look _____.

4. My teacher seems _____ by the end of each week.

5. The cartoons were _____.

6. This river is _____.

7. One beagle became _____.

8. The ocean may be _____ during the fierce storm.

9. Their movie must have been _____.

146

A predicate adjective occurs after the verb *and* ***goes back to <u>describe</u> <u>the subject</u> of the sentence.***

Remember: To have a predicate adjective, the sentence must contain a linking verb.

Linking Verbs:

to feel	to smell	to grow	to stay
to taste	to seem	to remain	to become
to look	to sound	to appear	to be (is, am, are, was, were, be, being, been)

                                                           P.A.
Example: The <u>skin</u> ~~of a hippopotamus~~ <u>looks</u> thick.   *thick* skin

🙐🙐🙐🙐🙐🙐🙐🙐🙐🙐🙐🙐🙐🙐🙐🙐🙐🙐

Directions: Write a predicate adjective in the blank.   Underline the subject once and the verb twice. Label the predicate adjective – **P.A.** Write the predicate adjective and the subject of the sentence in the blank following the sentence.

Example: Your <u>hair</u> <u>is</u> shiny.   *shiny* hair

1. That man is _____.   _____

2. These weights are _____.   _____

3. His sister seems _____.   _____

4. Their ideas sound _____.   _____

5. Your pet looks _____.   _____

6. This drink tastes _____.   _____

7. One child remained _____.   _____

DEGREES OF ADJECTIVES

We can say that someone is strong.   ➷   I am strong.

We may want **to compare two** objects or people.   ➷   You are strong**er** than I am.

We may want **to compare more than two**.   ➷   You are strong**est** in your family.

We use degrees of adjectives when we compare:
> *strong*
> *stronger*   =   **comparative degree** – comparing **2**
> *strongest*   =   **superlative degree** – comparing **3 or more**

COMPARATIVE DEGREE:

Rule A: **When comparing 2, add <u>er</u> to most one-syllable words.**

> Examples: soft – **softer**   brave – **braver**

Rule B: **When comparing 2, the word may totally change for a <u>few</u> one-syllable words.**

> Examples: good – **better**   bad – **worse**

Rule C: **When comparing 2, use <u>er</u> with some two-syllable words. Use a dictionary if necessary.**

> Examples: happy – **happier**   lively – **livelier**

Rule D: **When comparing 2, use <u>more</u> (or *less*) with most words of two or more syllables.**

> Examples: handsome – **more** handsome   demanding – **more** demanding

SUPERLATIVE DEGREE:

Rule A: **When comparing 3 or more, add <u>est</u> to most one-syllable words.**

> Examples: soft – **softest**   brave – **bravest**

Rule B: **When comparing 3 or more, the word may change for a <u>few</u> one-syllable words.**

> Examples: good – **best**   bad – **worst**

Rule C: **When comparing 3 or more, use <u>est</u> with some two-syllable words. Use a dictionary if necessary.**

> Examples: happy – **happiest**   lively – **liveliest**

Rule D: **When comparing 3 or more, use <u>most</u> (or *least*) with many words of two or more syllables. Use a dictionary if necessary.**

> Examples: handsome – **most** handsome   demanding – **most** demanding

ONE-SYLLABLE WORDS:

Comparing 2:   Use **er** most of the time.   ❀Your trophy is bigg**er** than mine.

Comparing 3 or more: Use **est** most of the time.   ❀Our team's trophy is biggest of all.

TWO-SYLLABLE WORDS:

Comparing 2:   Use **er** some of the time.   ❀The second story was <u>funni**er**</u> than the first.

Use **more** with many two-syllable words.   ❀I was **more** <u>upset</u> than my friend.

Comparing 3 or more: Use **est** some of the time.   ❀Of the ten comics, she was <u>funni**est**</u>.

Use **most** with many two-syllable words.

❀Of the four guides, our guide was **most** interesting.

THREE-SYLLABLE WORDS (OR MORE THAN THREE SYLLABLES):

Comparing 2:   Use **more** with words containing three or more syllables.

❀The second math problem was **more** <u>confusing</u> than the first.

Comparing 3 or more: Use **most** with words containing three or more syllables.

❀This math problem was **most** confusing of the entire worksheet.

కొ కొ కొ కొ కొ కొ కొ కొ కొ కొ కొ కొ కొ కొ కొ కొ

Directions: Circle the correct adjective.

1. A.   This shoe box is (larger, largest) than that plastic one.

B.   This shoebox is (larger, largest) of all the store's boxes.

2. A.   Your horse seems (calmer, calmest) than mine.

B.   Your horse seems (calmer, calmest) of all the horses in your corral.

3. A.   Her diamond ring is (shinier, shiniest) than her ruby ring.

B.   Her diamond ring is the (shinier, shiniest) jewelry she owns.

4. A.   This four-year-old is a (better, best) cutter than her little brother.

B.   This four-year-old is the (better, best) cutter in her preschool class.

Name_____   **ADJECTIVES**

Date_____   **Degrees of Adjectives**

ONE-SYLLABLE WORDS:

Comparing 2:   Use **er** most of the time.   ❀Bo is fast**er** than his son.

Comparing 3 or more: Use **est** most of the time.   ❀His son is fast**est** on his team.

TWO-SYLLABLE WORDS:

Comparing 2:   Use **er** some of the time.   ❀This kitten is friski**er** than its mother.

Use **more** with many two-syllable words.   ❀He was **more** careful than I was.

Comparing 3 or more: Use **est** some of the time.   ❀Your costume is scari**est** of all.

Use **most** with many two-syllable words.

❀Of the ten trails, the bike trail is **most** challenging.

THREE-SYLLABLE WORDS (OR MORE THAN THREE SYLLABLES):

Comparing 2:   Use **more** with many two-syllable words.

❀This can opener is **more** dependable than our old one.

Comparing 3 or more: Use **most** with many two-syllable words.

❀Of all of our appliances, our stove is **most** dependable.

ॐ ॐ ॐ ॐ ॐ ॐ ॐ ॐ ॐ ॐ ॐ ॐ ॐ ॐ ॐ ॐ ॐ

Directions: Circle the correct answer.

1. A.   Jana is the (more outgoing, most outgoing) twin.

B.   Tate is the (more outgoing, most outgoing) triplet.

2. A.   This yellow enamel egg is (lovelier, loveliest) than a plain glass egg.

B.   This yellow enamel egg is (lovelier, loveliest) of the entire egg collection.

3. A.   This performer seemed (more confident, most confident) than the first.

B.   The sixth performer seemed (more confident, most confident).

4. A.   These flat shoes are (more comfortable, most comfortable) than heels.

B.   These flat shoes are my (more comfortable, most comfortable) footwear.

150

ADJECTIVES

Degrees of Adjectives

Directions: Circle the correct degree of adjective.

1. This flavored iced tea is (tastier, tastiest) than the regular iced tea.

2. Your suggestion seems (more workable, most workable) than mine.

3. This puppy has the (smaller, smallest) paws of the entire litter.

4. Of their seven children, Kim is (more athletic, most athletic).

5. Of the two solutions, this one is (causticer, more caustic).

6. That roast is the (fresher, freshest) meat in the market.

7. This dirt trail is (more dangerous, most dangerous) of all the trails.

8. Today has been (hotter, hottest) than yesterday.

9. This room's carpet is the (more stained, most stained) rug in our house.

10. Your last message was (more concise, most concise) than your first.

11. My salad dressing seems (spicier, spiciest) than your honey-mustard one.

12. That round window appears (clearer, clearest) than the square one beside it.

13. A down jacket is (heavier, heaviest) than a windbreaker.

14. This china dish has the (more beautiful, most beautiful) pattern of the four.

15. Your second choice appears to be (more acceptable, most acceptable).

16. Our teacher seems the (quieter, quietest) person in the entire school.

17. Chan is the (more outspoken, most outspoken) triplet.

18. He is the (better, best) speller in our class.

Name_____   **ADJECTIVES**

Date_____   **Degrees of Adjectives**

Directions: Write the correct degree of adjective.

       Example: Our second helicopter ride was (bumpy) _____*bumpier*_____ .

1. An apple is a (healthy) _____ snack than a brownie.

2. Although I found six sea shells, this one is (good) _____.

3. The small cut on your arm is (deep) _____ than the cut on your leg .

4. Tim is the (popular) _____ uncle of the three.

5. Of the two drawers, this one is (organized) _____.

6. In the pack of rubber bands, this one was (flexible) _____.

7. The third garbage can smelled (bad) _____.

8. He is the (active) _____ member of the club.

9. An emerald is (precious) _____ than a garnet.

10. The dentist was (concerned) _____ about her third patient.

11. Of all the girls in her family, she seems (curious) _____.

12. Her parents are (young) _____ than mine.

13. Ezra is the (cooperative) _____ triplet.

14. This story is (tragic) _____ than the poem about the same subject.

15. I was (thrilled) _____ with my science grade than my math grade.

16. The office manager is (serious) _____ than the owner.

152

A. DESCRIPTIVE ADJECTIVES:

Directions: Write a descriptive adjective in each blank. Draw an arrow from the descriptive adjective to the noun it modifies (goes over to).

1. This _____ shirt looks new.

2. Would you like a (an) _____ roll?

3. A (An) _____ ship anchored off the coast.

4. We found that _____ bed in the attic.

5. Did you attend a (an) _____ show?

6. _____ lights have been installed.

ৡৡৡৡৡৡৡৡৡৡৡৡৡ

B. Limiting (Determining) Adjectives:

Articles: a, an, the

Demonstratives: this, that, these, those

Numbers: Example: *nine* baskets

Possessive Pronouns: my, his, her, your, its, our, their, whose

Possessive Nouns: Example: *animals'* tracks

Indefinites: any, few, no, many, most, several, some

Directions: Write an appropriate limiting adjective from each category.

1. **Article** – _____ peach is juicy.

Demonstratives – May I have _____ eraser.

Numbers – They own _____ sheep.

Possessive pronouns – _____ ankles are swollen.

Possessive nouns – Tara drew _____ picture.

Indefinites – _____ sunflowers have been planted.

C. Limiting Adjectives:

Remember: Some words can be limiting adjectives if they modify a noun. That same word will not be a limiting adjective if it stands alone.

Examples: Do you have **any** straws?   Adjective – *any* straws

I don't have ***any***.   *Any* what? We don't know. *Any* is not an adjective.

Directions: Place a ✓ in the blank if the boldfaced word is a limiting (determining) adjective. If the word is as an adjective, write the boldfaced word and the noun that it modifies (goes over to) in the wide blank.

1. ___   **Your** window is cracked. _____

2. ___   He made **few** errors on the test. _____

3. ___   Did we order **these**? _____

4. ___   Have you read **Tim's** newspaper article? _____

5. ___   I would like **four** in the pink color. _____

ംഛംഛംഛംഛംഛംഛംഛംഛംഛ

D. Proper Adjectives:

A proper adjective is a descriptive word. A proper adjective is **capitalized**.

Germany (noun)   a **G**erman watch

Directions: Circle any proper adjective. Draw an arrow to the word it modifies.

1. An Atlanta taxi took the couple to their hotel.

2. An Indian company makes these computers.

3. Have you visited a Jackson Hole ranch?

4. Is a macaw a South American bird?

E. **Predicate Adjectives:**
Sometimes an adjective occurs after the verb but describes the subject.
This is called a predicate adjective.

Directions: Cross out any prepositional phrases. Underline the subject once and the verb twice. Label the predicate adjective – **P.A.**

1.   My tennis shoes are soggy.

2.   That cottage near the pond is run-down.

3.   The ink is smudged on this paper.

4.   The clown's face looks frightening to some children.

🦂🦂🦂🦂🦂🦂🦂🦂🦂🦂🦂

F. **Degrees of Adjectives:**
Directions: Circle the correct answer.

1.   This circular saw seems (sharper, sharpest) than my hand saw.

2.   This car is (more compact, compacter) than the blue one.

3.   My cotton shirt is (more wrinkled, wrinkleder) than my silk one.

4.   Her attitude was (best, better) on her third day of work.

5.   Emma is the (more active, most active) woman in her exercise class.

🦂🦂🦂🦂🦂🦂🦂🦂🦂🦂🦂

G. **Identifying Adjectives:**
Directions: Circle any adjectives.

1.   No sweet corn floated in our chicken soup.

2.   Rustic, wooden beams were nailed on a plastered ceiling.

3.   We prepared crisp, Belgian waffles for those hungry guests.

4.   A glazed gray mirror broke into many jagged pieces.

A. **Prepositions and Object of the Preposition:**
    Directions: Cross out any prepositional phrases. Write **O.P.** above any
                  object of the preposition.

1.   The lamp with a leather shade sold for ten dollars.

2.   That pearl ring with diamonds on each side is pretty.

3.   She travels without shampoo or hair conditioner.

~~~~~~~~~~~~~

B. **Subject/Verb:**
    Directions: Cross out any prepositional phrases. Underline the subject once
                  and the verb twice.

1.   A small, steel ball rolled through the machine.

2.   One of the drivers stopped before the intersection.

3.   During the ice storm, several branches fell from a huge tree.

~~~~~~~~~~~~~

C. **Compound Subjects:**
    Directions: Cross out any prepositional phrases. Underline the subject once
                  and the verb or verb phrase twice.

1.   Sandy and her mother refinish old furniture.

2.   The jockey and the horse owner spoke with the press.

3.   Beans and tomato plants had been fertilized.

~~~~~~~~~~~~~

D. **Compound Verbs:**
    Directions: Cross out any prepositional phrases. Underline the subject once
                  and the verb or verb phrase twice.

1.   A father penguin sat and protected an egg.

2.   I sprinkled lemon on fish and placed the dish under a broiler.

3.   Mr. and Mrs. Ming must accept the offer, write a new contract, or cancel it.

E. **Infinitives:**

Directions: Cross out any prepositional phrases. Place parentheses **( )** around any infinitive. Underline the subject once and the verb twice.

1. The carpenter wants to build a cabin by a shallow stream.

2. I need to clean beneath the refrigerator.

3. The barber decided to leave early.

ক্ষ্ণ্ন্ক্ষ্ণ্ন্ক্ষ্ণ্ন্ক্ষ্ণ্ন্ক্ষ্ণ্ন্ক্ষ্ণ্ন্ক্ষ্ণ্ন

F. **Subject-Verb Agreement:**

Directions: Delete any prepositional phrases. Underline the subject once. Underline the verb/verb phrase that agrees with the subject twice.

1. That man (buy, buys) trucks through the Internet.

2. Streaks of orange and blue (crosses, cross) the sky.

3. African art (was, were) displayed in the building's lobby.

4. An Art Deco hotel (are, is) located within Paris.

5. My grandma (does[n't]), do[n't]) like to swim.

6. Bo and his sister (keep, keeps) bees for a living.

7. Everyone in those shops (work, works) late.

ক্ষ্ণ্ন্ক্ষ্ণ্ন্ক্ষ্ণ্ন্ক্ষ্ণ্ন্ক্ষ্ণ্ন্ক্ষ্ণ্ন্ক্ষ্ণ্ন

G. **Verb Phrases and *Not*:**

Directions: Cross out any prepositional phrases. Box *not* or *n't*. Underline the subject once and the verb or verb phrase twice.

1. I cannot write in this small space.

2. Sally will not shop without her husband.

3. This yellow highlighter doesn't have a cap.

H. **Contractions:**
     Directions: Write the contraction.

1. do not - _____   6. is not - _____

2. I am - _____   7. I have - _____

3. where is -_____   8. she is - _____

4. you are - _____   9. will not - _____

5. could not - _____   10. I would - _____

ฅฅฅฅฅฅฅฅฅฅฅฅ

I. **You're/Your, It's/Its, and They're/Their/There:**
     Directions: Circle the correct word.

1. The door is off (it's, its) hinges.

2. (You're, Your) knuckle appears bruised.

3. Val and I met (they're, their, there).

ฅฅฅฅฅฅฅฅฅฅฅฅ

J. **Auxiliary (Helping) Verbs:**
     Directions: Write the 23 helping verbs.

1. *D's*   a. _____   b. _____   c. _____

2. *H's*   a. _____   b. _____   c. _____

3. *M's*   a. _____   b. _____   c. _____

4. *Ould's*   a. _____   b. _____   c. _____

5. *To be:*   a. _____   c. _____   e. _____   g. _____

              b. _____   d. _____   f. _____   h. _____

6. *Others:*   a. _____   b. _____   c. _____

158

K. **Irregular Verbs:**
   Directions: Underline the subject once and the correct verb phrase twice.

1. A dam must have (burst, bursted).

2. Your pizza has (came, come).

3. Had she (done, did) a science project?

4. I should have (ate, eaten) kiwi.

5. The pond is now (frozen, froze).

6. These guitar strings are (broke, broken).

7. A portrait has been (hanged, hung).

8. That teenager has (drove, driven) his own car.

        🙞🙞🙞🙞🙞🙞🙞🙞🙞🙞🙞🙞🙞

L. **Subjects, Verbs, and Direct Objects:**
   Directions: Cross out any prepositional phrases. Underline the subject once
                 and the verb/verb phrase twice. Label any direct object – **D.O.**

1. The walker crossed a bridge near a waterwheel.

2. Does Loni make silver rings with emeralds?

3. We placed a wagon wheel by our fireplace.

        🙞🙞🙞🙞🙞🙞🙞🙞🙞🙞🙞🙞🙞

M. **Sit/Set, Lie/Lay, and Rise/Raise:**
   Directions: Delete any prepositional phrases. Underline the subject once
                 and the verb/verb phrase twice. Label any direct object – **D.O.**

1. (Lie, Lay) down.   4.   He (sits, sets) barrels on a dock.

2. (Sit, Set) here.   5.   A box has (laid, lain) there for weeks.

3. (Rise, Raise) your hand.   6.   The dog (rose, raised) slowly.

N. **Tenses:**

Directions: Underline the subject once and the verb or verb phrase twice. Write the tense (*present, past,* or *future*) in the blank.

1. _____ He irons well.

2. _____ Chris clapped for his favorite wrestler.

3. _____ A minister will perform the marriage ceremony.

4. _____ Several mules are thirsty.

5. _____ One polo player leaned over his horse.

ൟൟൟൟൟൟൟൟൟൟൟ

O. **Linking Verbs:**

Directions: Unscramble these linking verbs.

1. (to) aminer - _____   5. (to) leslm - _____   9. (to) mese - _____

2. (to) oklo - _____   6. (to) worg - _____   10. (to) prapae - _____

3. (to) eatts - _____   7. (to) lefe - _____   11. (to) ytas _____

4. to emcbeo - _____   8. (to) dosun - _____   12. (to) eb - _____

a. si - _____   b. ma - _____   c. rea - _____   d. asw - _____

e. rewe - _____   f. eb - _____   g. gnieb - _____   h. eneb - _____

ൟൟൟൟൟൟൟൟൟൟൟ

P. **Action Verb or Linking Verb?:**

Directions: Place **X** if the verb is linking.

1. _____ The garlic **smelled** strong.

2. _____ He **smelled** the garlic.

3. _____ Her hair **looks** purple.

4. _____ She **looks** for vintage pins.

Q. **Transitive and Intransitive Verbs:**

Directions: Underline the subject once and the verb or verb phrase twice. Label any direct object – **D.O.** Write **T** if the verb is transitive; write **I** if the verb is intransitive.

Remember: A transitive verb will have a direct object.

D.O.T. > Direct **O**bject = **T**ransitive

1. _____   The housecleaner scoured the dirty tub.

2. _____   Joy filled a children's swimming pool.

3. _____   He speaks very softly.

୬ଈ୬ଈ୬ଈ୬ଈ୬ଈ୬ଈ୬ଈ୬ଈ୬ଈ୬ଈ

R. **Abstract and Concrete Nouns:**

Directions: Place a ⚥ if the noun is abstract.

1. ____	ANTLER		5. ____	WELCOME
2. ____	STRAP		6. ____	DOMINO
3. ____	COMFORT		7. ____	FONDNESS
4. ____	STRESS		8. ____	OUTLET

୬ଈ୬ଈ୬ଈ୬ଈ୬ଈ୬ଈ୬ଈ୬ଈ୬ଈ୬ଈ

S. **Singular and Plural Nouns:**

Directions: Write the correct spelling of each plural noun.

1. valley - _____	6. identity - _____
2. range - _____	7. crutch - _____
3. chief - _____	8. news - _____
4. scene - _____	9. bluff - _____
5. cargo - _____	10. harness - _____

T. **Possessive Nouns:**
Directions: Write the possessive and the item(s) owned in each blank.

1. the temperature for today - _____

2. signs owned by a company - _____

3. a stroller for two infants - _____

🚲🚲🚲🚲🚲🚲🚲🚲🚲🚲🚲🚲

U. **Nouns Used as Subjects, Direct Objects, and Indirect Objects:**
Directions: Label any subject (**S.**), direct object (**D.O.**), and indirect object (**I.O.**).

1. An architect handed his client the building plans.

🚲🚲🚲🚲🚲🚲🚲🚲🚲🚲🚲🚲

V. **Predicate Nominatives:**
Directions: Underline the subject once and the verb twice. Label a predicate nominative – **P.N.** Write the inverted form in the blank.
Remember: A predicate nominative occurs _after_ a linking verb and means the same as the subject.

1. My father's dentist was Dr. Lucash.

_____

2. An old inn is their new home.

_____

🚲🚲🚲🚲🚲🚲🚲🚲🚲🚲🚲🚲

W. **Identifying Nouns:**
Directions: Circle any nouns.
Remember: Determiners will help you to find some nouns.

1. Three lawnmowers were sold at that pawn shop.

2. Jake's uncle has no mirrors in his house.

3. Nanny made thirteen yellow costumes for her first dance performance.

162

Name_____   **ADJECTIVES**

Date_____   **Used in Writing**

Adjectives are extremely important in writing. They add description and detail.

Directions: Insert an adjective in each blank. Be sure that your adjectives are descriptive. Be creative!

1.   The woman is wearing a (an) _____ dress. It has

_____ sequins and _____ beads on the

skirt. The hem is trimmed with _____ lace. The sleeves

are _____. What a (an) _____

garment!

2.   The hiker is wearing a (an) _____ jacket. It has

_____ sleeves and _____ buttons.

The collar is trimmed with _____ leather. The

_____ fabric seems _____.

3.   A vehicle has been reported stolen. It is a (an) _____

car with _____ paint . It has _____ tires

with _____ rims. The fender is _____. The

windows are _____. This vehicle is very _____.

Adjectives are extremely important in writing.

It is important to use a thesaurus.   This will help you to find vivid descriptors. It also helps to prevent you from overusing an adjective.

Directions: Use a thesaurus. Replace each boldfaced adjective.

1.   We heard a (**loud**) _____ noise.

2.   This blanket is (**dirty**) _____.

3.   A (**wet**) _____ cloth is lying on the kitchen counter.

4.   The child was (**bad**) _____.

5.   The teenager seemed (**unhappy**) _____ about her friends' decision.

6.   May I have a glass of (**cold**) _____ water?

7.   The man was dressed in (**torn**) _____ denim pants.

8.   Take this (**smelly**) _____ trash out.

9.   A (**good**) _____ artist has displayed his work.

10.   That rock is (**big**) _____.

11.   My new calculator is (**small**) _____.

12.   His sister is (**nice**) _____.

13.   This story is (**interesting**) _____.

14.   The woman's (**funny**) _____ presentation made us laugh.

15.   Your sponge is (**soft**) _____.

ADVERBS

VERBS

Note that the word, *ADVERBS*, contains the word, *VERBS*. This should help you to remember that most adverbs modify, or go over to, the verb in a sentence.

Adverbs that tell how, when, or where usually modify a verb.

	Adv.	
Examples:	A <u>ladybug</u> <u>moved</u> slowly.	(*how*)
	Adv.	
	A <u>ladybug</u> <u>landed</u> suddenly.	(*when*)
	Adv.	
	A <u>ladybug</u> <u>flew</u> away.	(*where*)

Most adverbs that tell *how* end in ly.

Examples:	fresh**ly**	beautiful**ly**	careless**ly**
	local**ly**	bold**ly**	sure**ly**

Adjectives such as *hard* and *fast* can be adverbs that tell **how**.

> We worked **hard** selling granola bars.
> They ate their lunch **fast**.

Beware: There are some adjectives that end in *ly*: friendly   lovely

Some adverbs tell *to what extent*. There are seven adverbs that are used frequently to tell *to what extent (how much)*.

not   so   very   too   quite   rather   somewhat

<u>If you memorize these, you can easily find them in a sentence.</u>

Of course, other words can tell *to what extent*.

> Tate is *totally* frustrated by the unusual directions.
> Tate is *completely* frustrated by the unusual directions.

An adverb is a word that can tell <u>when</u>.

Directions: In Part A, delete any prepositional phrase(s). Underline the subject once and the verb or verb phrase twice. Label each adverb – *Adv.* Fill in the blanks in Part B.

Adv.

Example: A.   <u>We</u> often <u>swim</u> in a lake.

B.   _____*Often*_____ tells _*when*_ we ____*swim*____.

1. A.   They recently moved to the country.

B.   _____ tells _____ they _____.

2. A.   A band will perform tonight after dark.

B.   _____ tells _____ a band _____.

3. A.   We are leaving tomorrow before breakfast.

B.   _____ tells _____ we _____.

4. A.   One teacher arrived late to math class.

B.   _____ tells _____ one teacher _____.

5. A.   The board meets daily.

B.   _____ tells _____ the board _____.

6. A.   Our grandmother occasionally gives a tea for her friends.

B.   _____ tells _____ our grandmother _____.

7. A.   My doctor frequently laughs.

B.   _____ tells _____ my doctor _____.

An adverb is a word that can tell *when*.

Directions: Delete any prepositional phrases. Underline the subject once
and the verb or verb phrase twice. Label each adverb – *Adv.*
Write the verb and the adverb on the line.

                                    Adv.
        Example: His <u>dog</u> frequently <u>jumps</u> ~~on visitors~~.   **jumps frequently**

1. Jemima sat by a pool today. _____

2. He might compete against his cousin later. _____

3. Tara always wears bright colors. _____

4. Do you ever skate with your cousins? _____

5. I must buy my ticket now. _____

6. Pedro sometimes parks his bike by these trees. _____

7. That woman visits her mother monthly. _____

8. He would never agree to do that. _____

9. Their flight will arrive late. _____

10. Tim may come with me tomorrow after school. _____

11. My uncle often buys old tools at auctions. _____

12. I should have washed my hair earlier. _____

13. Her parents write a letter to the editor weekly. _____

14. Recently, Emma hiked near a stable. _____

15. Call me soon. _____

An adverb is a word that can tell <u>where</u>.

Directions: Think about words that can tell where. Fill in the blanks to spell adverbs that tell *where*.

1. i _

2. o _

3. u _

4. d _ w _

5. i _ s _ d _

6. o _ f

7. o _ t s _ d _

8. t h r _ u _ h

9. h _ r _

10. t _ e _ e

11. a _ _ w _ e _ e

12. n _ w _ e r _

13. s _ m e _ h _ r _

14. e _ e _ y _ h _ r e

15. d _ w _ t _ w n

16. _ w _ y

17. f _ r w _ r d

18. a _ o u _ d

168

An adverb is a word that can tell _where_.

Directions: In Part A, delete any prepositional phrase(s). Underline the
subject once and the verb or verb phrase twice. Label each
adverb – _Adv._ Fill in the blanks in Part B.

Adv.

Example: A.   The girl ~~with the furry dog~~ plays close ~~to her home~~.

B.   ___Close___ tells _where_ the girl _plays_.

1. A.   A mole lives here.

B.   _____ tells _____ a mole _____.

2. A.   I went nowhere after my dental appointment.

B.   _____ tells _____ I _____.

3. A.   There is Carlos!

B.   _____ tells _____ Carlos _____.

4. A.   That lamp leans forward.

B.   _____ tells _____ the lamp _____.

5. A.   One of the racers threw a towel up in the air.

B.   _____ tells _____ one _____.

6. A.   His grandpa walks downtown for a newspaper.

B.   _____ tells _____ his grandpa _____.

7. A.   Her boots are outside beside the back door.

B.   _____ tells _____ her boots _____.

8. A.   A bird flew by with a twig in its beak.

B.   _____ tells _____ a bird _____.

An adverb is a word that can tell *where*.

Directions: Delete any prepositional phrase(s). Underline the subject once and
                    the verb or verb phrase twice. Label each adverb – *Adv.*

1. Dr. Silversmith laid his cellular phone down.

2. Loni waded upstream.

3. His cat rolled over on its side.

4. You may move forward.

5. Their dog runs around in circles.

6. Does Carla live nearby?

7. They went outside after the downpour.

8. Are you going far?

9. Some children hopped sideways during the game.

10. Two swimmers pushed away from the side of a pool.

11. You should have come inside before the snowstorm.

12. Both Gretta and her brother will join us there.

13. Many of the surfers rushed out to catch waves.

14. Come aboard.

Adverbs can tell *how*.

Directions: Unscramble these adverbs that tell *how*.

1. lystof - _ _ _ _ _ _

2. lyftisw - _ _ _ _ _ _ _

3. lygthit - _ _ _ _ _ _ _

4. lyldiw - _ _ _ _ _ _

5. lyewets - _ _ _ _ _ _ _

6. lysprah - _ _ _ _ _ _ _

7. llew - _ _ _ _

8. lypeasntla - _ _ _ _ _ _ _ _ _ _

9. lylys - _ _ _ _ _

10. lyuiqte - _ _ _ _ _ _ _

11. lypoheful - _ _ _ _ _ _ _ _ _

12. lydlou - _ _ _ _ _ _

13. lyandregsou - _ _ _ _ _ _ _ _ _ _ _   171

Adverbs can tell *how*.

Directions: Write an adverb that tells *how* in each blank. Do not reuse an
             adverb.

1. You did that _____.

2. Those teenage boys are throwing horseshoes _____.

3. His neighbor drives _____.

4. Stop acting _____.

5. Tate waved _____.

6. We ate _____.

7. They build campfires _____.

8. Jonah rolled a cart _____.

9. A small snake slid _____ down a rock.

10. Kalani shook the rug _____.

11. Those children play _____.

12. That student studies _____.

13. The winner of the contest smiled _____.

14. Some of the birds flew _____.

15. Fry our bacon _____, please.

16. Press the elevator button _____.

17. A lifeguard yelled _____ to several swimmers.

Directions: Delete any prepositional phrases. Underline the subject once and the verb or verb phrase twice. Circle any adverb that tells *how*.

1. Rain slid quietly down the window.

2. The truck stopped carefully at a traffic light.

3. Pierre blew bubbles gleefully.

4. One child talked eagerly about his hike.

5. Several beagles lay peacefully under a tree.

6. My father mixed butter and eggs together.

7. A band marched fast during the parade.

8. This fire in our fireplace is burning brightly.

9. The grandpa rocked the baby gently and sang.

10. Dora and Tom scribbled their notes rapidly.

11. Sand blew strongly across the desert.

12. Carlo sanded wood smoothly for a cutting board.

13. One of the bowlers throws her bowling ball hesitantly.

14. Did Lars finish the puzzle completely?

15. Rinse these dishes well with warm water.

ADVERB or ADJECTIVE?

Have you heard anyone say the following sentence?

♦**Incorrect**:   **You are acting strange.**

Acting is an **action** verb. You must use an **adverb** that tells how you are acting.

☺   **Correct**:   **You *are acting* strangely.**

However, if the verb is a linking verb (not action), use an adjective.

☺   **Correct**:   **I *look* strange in this costume.**

A review of linking verbs may help you!

Linking verbs do **not** show action; they usually make a statement.

to feel	to smell	to grow	to stay
to taste	to seem	to remain	to become
to look	to sound	to appear	to be (is, am, are, was, were, be, being, been)

Example: His leg <u>cast</u> <u>looks</u> frayed.

To look is on the linking verb list. Replacing *looks* with *is* does not change the meaning of the sentence.

                                                    is
Example: His leg cast <u>looks</u> frayed.

After a linking verb, use an adjective. This adjective will be a <u>describing word</u>.

My soup is **excellent**.   (adjective – excellent soup)
You spell **excellently**.   (adverb – telling *how* you spell)

| *Adjective* | *Adverb* |
| fine | finely |

Examples:

My health is <u>fine</u>.

I <u>chopped</u> the celery <u>finely</u>.
**action
verb**   **how?**

respectful

respectfully

The child is very <u>respectful</u>.

<u>Ask</u> me <u>respectfully</u>.
action   how?
verb

bad

badly

He feels <u>bad</u>.

I <u>played</u> golf <u>badly</u> today.
action   how?
verb

good

well*

Their fort is <u>good</u>.

He <u>races</u> go-carts <u>well</u>.
action   how?
Verb

*When using an action verb *and* telling <u>how</u>, use *well*, not *good*.
> Kent *makes* pottery well.
> Jana *skis* well.
> He *speaks* well.
> Margie *drove* the speed boat well.

Remember that ***fast*** and ***hard*** are the same in the adjective form and the adverb form.

Examples:	<u>fast</u>	That train is **fast**.	(adjective)
		You move **fast**.	(adverb)
	<u>hard</u>	This is a **hard** question.	(adjective)
		You work **hard**.	(adverb)

175

Directions: Write the adverb form of the boldfaced adjective.

1. Jana is a **quick** painter. She painted the room _____.

2. Josh has a **quiet** voice. He speaks _____.

3. That girl is very **shy**. She smiles _____ at us.

4. This wood project is **hard**. I'm working _____ on it.

5. The rider was **silent**. She rode _____.

6. This bench is **solid**. It has been built _____.

7. The witness was **nervous**. He answered _____.

8. Our teacher looked **tired**. She nodded _____.

9. My neighbor is an **excellent** cook. He cooks _____.

10. Mario is a **good** dancer. He dances _____.

11. The sailboat is a **fast** boat. It moves _____.

12. His doctor is **kind**. He deals _____ with his patients.

13. Joe and Mona are **brave**. They skydive _____.

14. The first grader is a **careful** printer. He prints _____.

15. That vehicle is **slow**. It's moving _____ up a steep hill.

Adverbs change the meaning of a sentence.

Directions: Write 2 different adverbs that tell *how* in each blank. Do not reuse an adverb.

1. The woman tapped _____ on the car window.

    _____

2. Two workers discussed the problem _____.

    _____

3. Many children played _____ in a wading pool.

    _____

4. He always rows _____ across the local lake.

    _____

5. A bear ate _____ from a garbage can.

    _____

6. Toni often plays chess _____.

    _____

7. They dress _____ for some occasions.

    _____

8. The shopper crossed the street _____.

    _____

Directions: Write the adverb form of the boldfaced adjective.

1. **distinct** ~   The guide speaks _____.

2. **proud** ~   They salute the flag _____.

3. **sad** ~   Several friends said goodbye _____.

4. **illegal** ~   The driver made a U-turn _____.

5. **main** ~   Her father works _____ as a tuna fisher.

6. **good** ~   The teenagers are surfing _____.

7. **secure** ~   Your package has been tied _____.

8. **silent** ~   Some workers waited _____ for a bus.

9. **loose** ~   Large boards hung _____ on the old barn.

10. **bad** ~   I sprained my ankle _____ yesterday.

11. **hard** ~   Chessa kicked the ball _____ into the goal.

12. **furious** ~   Their dog barked _____ at the passing motorists.

13. **complete** ~   Please fill out the form _____.

14. **brilliant** ~   A harvest moon shines _____.

15. **sleepy** ~   The toddler _____ mumbled good night.

16. **truthful** ~   He answered the judge _____.

17. **awkward** ~   In his first attempt, the new-born colt stood _____.

Name_____   **ADVERBS**

Date_____   **How, When, Where**

A. Directions: In Part A, write an adverb telling *how, when,* or *where.*
                   In Part B, write what that adverb tells: *how, when,* or *where.*

1. Part A: Go _____.

    Part B: _____

2. Part A: I searched _____.

    Part B: _____

3. Part A: A chipmunk scurried _____.

    Part B: _____

4. Part A: We _____ arrive on time.

    Part B: _____

B. Directions: Cross out any prepositional phrases. Underline the subject
                   once and the verb or verb phrase twice. Circle the adverb.
                   In the blank, write if the adverb tells *how, when,* or *where.*

1. The department store closed early.   _____

2. Her charm bracelet rattled noisily.   _____

3. That mason works alone on Mondays.   _____

4. A crane set a huge crate down.   _____

5. Everyone exited immediately.   _____

6. We are going nowhere for vacation.   _____

7. Does this bus travel downtown?   _____

Name_____

Date_____

Most adverbs that tell *when, where,* or *how* modify (go over to) a verb.

Miss Arrow moved **there**.   *There tells <u>where</u> Miss Arrow moved.*
She moved **recently**.   *Recently tells <u>when</u> she moved.*
She moved **quickly**.   *Quickly tells <u>how</u> she moved.*

<u>Seven adverbs usually tell *to what extent*. There are others, like *really,* but these 7 are used most often.</u>

1   2   3   4   5   6   7
Not, so, very, too, quite, rather, somewhat

Adverbs that tell *to what extent* are harder to understand because they can modify (go over to) a <u>verb</u>, an <u>adjective</u>, or even another <u>adverb</u>.

Examples:

I did **not** go.   (modifies a verb)
This poem is **rather** long.   (modifies *long,* an adjective)
She walks **very** cautiously on crutches. (modifies *cautiously,* an adverb that tells <u>how</u>)

ର୍ଶର୍ଶର୍ଶର୍ଶର୍ଶର୍ଶର୍ଶର୍ଶର୍ଶର୍ଶର୍ଶର୍ଶର୍ଶର୍ଶ

Directions: Unscramble the seven adverbs that often tell *to what extent*.

1. os - _ _

2. thsmaweo - _ _ _ _ _ _ _ _

3. etiqu - _ _ _ _ _

4. oto - _ _ _

5. herrta - _ _ _ _ _ _

6. revy - _ _ _ _

7. ont - _ _ _

Adverbs that tell *to what extent* can modify (go over to) a <u>verb</u>, an <u>adjective</u>, or even another <u>adverb</u>.

Not, so, very, too, quite, rather, somewhat

వేవేవేవేవేవేవేవేవేవేవేవేవేవేవేవేవే

Directions: Write an adverb that tells *to what extent*. Do not reuse an adverb.

1.   The patient's pulse was _____ weak.

2.   A librarian read _____ softly to the children.

3.   Her aim was _____ far to the left.

4.   Our city has become _____ large.

5.   This is _____ funny!

6.   The fountain bubbles _____ gently.

7.   Listen to this _____ scary tale.

వేవేవేవేవేవేవేవేవేవేవేవేవేవేవేవేవే

Other words such as *really* may also tell *to what extent*.

   Real is an adjective. That is a <u>real</u> muscle car.

   Really tells *to what extent*. Are you <u>really</u> hungry? (to what extent hungry?)

Directions: Circle the correct word:

1.   You must remain (real, really) quiet.

2.   I think that cartoon is (quiet, quite) silly.

3.   We walk (really, real) fast.

4.   Are you (real, really) strong?

Adverbs can tell *to what extent.*

Directions: Circle any adverbs that tell *to what extent.*

1.   Are you too wide-awake to sleep?

2.   The insect buzzed rather loudly around my head.

3.   Do not finish your task until tomorrow.

4.   We are really excited about going with our aunt to Georgia.

5.   She is somewhat afraid to voice her opinions.

6.   The program ended quite abruptly.

7.   My great-grandmother is so witty.

8.   I could barely hear his voice due to a loud noise.

9.   The pilot spoke very clearly to her passengers.

10.   My sister dresses quite smartly for work at her office.

11.   Her landlord was extremely perturbed about the leak in her roof.

12.   My mother is somewhat deaf in her left ear.

13.   Doesn't Jasmin go to dance class on Sundays?

14.   A very shy child peered quite timidly into a cardboard box.

15.   The creek rose rather swiftly during heavy rains.

16.   This lamp has been partially damaged by sun rays.

17.   My oatmeal is too thick and rather sugary.

Adverbs can tell *how, when, where,* or *to what extent.*

Adverbs that tell **how, when,** or **where** usually modify (go over to) a **verb**.

Adverbs that tell *to what extent* may modify a **verb**, an **adjective**, or another **adverb**.

❧❧❧❧❧❧❧❧❧❧❧❧❧❧❧❧❧❧

Directions: Circle any adverb in the sentence. The number in parentheses ( ) tells how many adverbs are in that sentence.

1. (2) We are going there today.

2. (3) Now and then, a mouse runs rapidly from its hole.

3. (2) We worked hard together on a social studies project.

4. (3) Omar sang loudly to a very lively crowd yesterday.

5. (2) Jana does not feel well.

6. (2) Jake kicked the ball hard and ran fast toward the goal.

7. (2) Several ranchers met here for a very short conference.

8. (3) Tomorrow, you must look somewhere for a rather old clock.

9. (2) I wrote my name so carefully on the dotted line.

Comparative and Superlative Degrees of Adverbs

To compare **2**, we use the **comparative degree**.

A.   One-syllable words usually add **er** to compare **2** things or people.

    Jodi runs fast.   Jodi runs fast**er** than her coach.

B.   Most two-syllable words use **more*** to compare **2**.

        The first speaker spoke loudly to the audience.

        The next speaker spoke **more** loudly than the first.

C.   Words of three or more syllables use **more*** to compare **2**.

    Joshua climbed carefully.   His sister climbed **more** carefully than he.

D.   Some words change forms to compare **2**.

    I played chess *badly* yesterday.   I played *worse* today.

                   ❧❧❧❧❧❧❧❧

To compare **3 or more**, we use the **superlative degree**.

A.   One-syllable words usually add **est** to compare **3 or more**.

        Jodi runs fast**est** of the entire team.

B.   Most two-syllable words use **most**** to compare **3 or more**.

       The last speaker spoke **most** loudly of all.

C.   Words of three or more syllables use **most**** to compare **3 or more**.

       He climbed down *most* carefully during his fifth try.

D.   Some words change forms to compare **3 or more**.

       I played chess *worst* during my fourth game.

*or less
**or least

184

Name_____   **ADVERBS**

Date_____   **Degrees**

Directions: In Part A, write the adverb form of the italicized word.
               In Part B, write the comparative or superlative form.

        Part A: *willing* - ___**willingly**___
        Part B: The fourth worker did the job ___**most willingly**___.

1. Part A: *sound* - _____

    Part B: I sleep _____ than my brother.

2. Part A: *quick* - _____

    Part B: I wrote my first email _____ than my
              second one.

3. Part A: *violent* - _____

    Part B: The third volcano erupted _____.

4. Part A: *close* - _____

    Part B: A jeweler looked at the second gem _____.

5. Part A: *soon* - _____

    Part B: Of the three students, Ellie finished _____.

6. Part A: *clear* - _____

    Part B: This large package is labeled _____ than
              the small one.

7. Part A: *dangerous* - _____

    Part B: The ship tilted _____during the third
              storm.

                                                                185

Directions: Circle the correct adverb form.

1. Of all the critics, he judges (more fairly, most fairly).

2. She laid the second board (more evenly, most evenly) than the first.

3. This brown puppy plays (more eagerly, most eagerly) than that white one.

4. Their grandpa rocked his fourth grandchild (longer, longest).

5. The wind is blowing (more fiercely, most fiercely) today than yesterday.

6. Pablo heeded the third signal (more quickly, most quickly).

7. The actress discussed her life (more frankly, most frankly) during her
    second interview.

8. Our team worked (more cooperatively, most cooperatively) than the other
    team.

9. Carlo cooks (more expertly, most expertly) of all the chefs.

10. The client responded (more favorably, most favorably) than her lawyer.

11. Of the two machines, this one spins (more safely, most safely).

12. Of the four customs agents, he answers questions (more willingly, most
    willingly).

13. Mr. Lu works (more steadily, most steadily) than his son.

14. The tallest triplet plays tennis (more boldly, most boldly).

15. Chan dresses (better, best) than his brother.

16. The woman petted the third fawn (more gently, most gently).

Directions: Circle the correct adverb form.

1. One photographer adjusted her lens (more exactly, most exactly) for the second shot.

2. A logger pulled the third rope (more snugly, most snugly).

3. The woman climbed (higher, highest) during her second try.

4. He swam (better, best) during his fourth race.

5. I do my exercises (more cheerfully, most cheerfully) than my mother.

6. Patrick spoke (more plainly, most plainly) during his second debate.

7. I turned the last of the four screws (more tightly, most tightly).

8. Pierre petted the second dog (more fearlessly, most fearlessly).

9. This car runs (more smoothly, most smoothly) than that van.

10. The taller twin throws a shot put (farther, farthest).

11. We rested (more often, most often) on our second hike in the state forest.

12. That candidate speaks (more freely, most freely) than his opponent.

13. The ambassador smiled (more warmly, most warmly) for the fifth picture.

14. Maria walks (more clumsily, most clumsily) in heels than in flat shoes.

15. Garth hung the second drape (more loosely, most loosely) than the first.

16. Of the triplets, Dakota lives (more simply, most simply).

17. Does a racer steer (better, best) than an antique roadster?

A. Adjectives and Adverbs:

Directions: Write the adverb form of each adjective.

1. A captain gave a **polite** answer.

    She answered _____.

2. They are **generous** givers.

    They give _____ to a charity.

3. It is a **compact** dishwasher.

    It fits _____ between the sink and refrigerator.

4. The actor wore a **shabby** outfit.

    The actor was dressed _____.

5. Kiki is a **fast** skier.

    Kiki skis _____.

B. Adjectives and Adverbs:

Directions: Write the adverb form of each adjective.

1. helpful - _____

2. restless - _____

3. childish - _____

4. grumpy - _____

5. awkward - _____

C. Adjectives and Adverbs:

Directions: Write the adverb form of the boldfaced adjective.

1. **quiet** ~ The child is playing _____ with her kitten.

2. **silent** ~ A horseman rode _____ into town.

3. **steady** ~ A young gymnast walked _____ along
      a beam.

4. **illegal** ~ The person crossed the street _____.

5. **recent** ~ We received an award _____.

6. **slight** ~ This package is _____ damaged.

7. **noisy** ~ The group walked _____ to the ballroom.

8. **slow** ~ You are building your model _____.

9. **calm** ~ The ducks waddled _____ toward the pond.

10. **bad** ~ I sprained my ankle _____.

11. **furious** ~ Their dog often barks _____.

12. **complete** ~ Please fill out this form _____.

13. **brilliant** ~ The sun shone _____.

14. **fast** ~ Several mustangs ran _____ toward the
      mountains.

15. **usual** ~ He is _____ very talkative in the morning.

D. Adverbs Telling *When*:

Directions: Write the adverb that means *when*.

> *Helpful Note:*   An antonym is a word that means the opposite.
> A synonym means the same or nearly the same.

1. an antonym for *sooner* - _____

2. means the same as *every day* - _____

3. "It's now or _____."

4. a word that means *this day* - _____

5. a synonym for always - _____

E. Adverbs Telling *When*:

Directions: Write three adverbs telling *when* that will make sense in each
sentence.

1. I want to go _____.

    _____.

    _____.

2. That child _____ takes a nap.

    _____

    _____

3. Do you _____ visit your grandparents?

    _____

    _____

F. Adverbs Telling *When*:

Directions: Delete (cross out) any prepositional phrases. Underline the subject once and the verb or verb phrase twice. Circle any adverb that tells *when*.

1. I never gargle with salt water.

2. A man in a choir gown suddenly turned to his neighbor.

3. During the World Series, her uncle pitched late in the last game.

4. One of the women at a swap meet always sells plastic sunglasses.

5. Jim and his sister deliver newspapers early.

G. Adverbs Telling *Where*:

Directions: Write three adverbs that tell *where* to complete each sentence. (Try to use a different adverb in all three sentences.)

1. Come   _____.

    _____.

    _____.

2. The jogger runs _____.

    _____.

    _____.

3. Stay   _____.

    _____.

    _____.

H. Adverbs Telling *How*:

Directions: Unscramble the adverb that tells *how*.

1.   Sit (p u) _____.

2.   I don't feel (l e w l) _____.

3.   The items on the belt at the grocery store moved (s y l w o l)

  _____.

4.   One fan yelled (l d u o y l) _____ for the losing

  team.

5.   The group worked (e r t h t o e g) _____.

I. Adverbs Telling *How*:

Directions: Delete (cross out) any prepositional phrases. Underline the subject
            once and the verb or verb phrase twice. Circle any adverb that tells
            how.

1. The waiter greeted us courteously.

2. An ice-cream vendor quickly handed a cone to the child.

3. Grandpa cooks and bakes well.

4. An air controller watches his instruments closely.

5. You must clean your drums thoroughly.

6. Before her long trip, the traveler studied her map carefully.

J. Adverbs Telling *To What Extent*:

Directions: Circle any adverb that tells *to what extent*.

1.   You are so talented.

2.   Press the cookies rather lightly with your hand.

3.   The toddler is not walking steadily.

4.   This gumbo is too thick and somewhat over-cooked.

5.   You sound quite sure of your decision.

K.   Degrees:

Directions: Circle the correct degree of each adverb.

1.   I didn't feel well yesterday, but today I feel (better, best).

2.   Of the four brothers, Stan visits his parents (more often, most often).

3.   The maid vacuumed (faster, fastest) on the second day of her new job.

4.   His fifth shirt fit into the luggage (more snugly, most snugly).

5.   Of the ten hot air balloons, the striped one climbed (higher, highest).

6.   The shortest triplet skips (more happily, most happily).

7.   In the law office, Luke types (more quickly, most quickly).

8.   Jill cleans the yard (more completely, most completely) than her sister.

A. **Prepositions and Object of the Preposition:**
      Directions: Cross out any prepositional phrases. Write **O.P.** above any
                          object of the preposition.

1.   The teenager in the red shirt works at a bookstore.

B. **Subject/Verb:**
      Directions: Cross out any prepositional phrases. Underline the subject once
                          and the verb twice.

1.   After shopping during the morning, I ate a salad.

2.   The mayor walked toward the town square with a group of shop owners.

C. **Compound Subjects and Verbs:**
      Directions: Cross out any prepositional phrases. Underline the subject once
                          and the verb or verb phrase twice.

1.   Sally asked for a glass of water and thanked the waiter.

2.   Their pet hamster ate, drank some water, and ran in circles around its cage.

D. **Subject-Verb Agreement:**
      Directions: Delete any prepositional phrases. Underline the subject once.
                          Underline the verb/verb phrase that agrees with the subject twice.

1.   His cousins (live, lives) near the Great Lakes.

2.   The girl in the white tennis shoes (was, were) the leader.

3.   She (take, takes) a trolley downtown.

E. **Contractions:**
      Directions: Write the contraction.

1. cannot - _____   3. we have - _____   5. they are - _____

2. will not - _____   4. I have - _____   6. what is - _____

F. **You're/Your, It's/Its, and They're/Their/There:**
    Directions: Circle the correct word.

1. (There, Their, They're) dog lost (it's, its) collar.

2. Do you know (you're, your) new address?

3. I know that (you're, your) going if (there, their, they're) buying the ticket.
        ༀༀༀༀༀༀༀༀༀༀༀༀ

G. **Auxiliary (Helping) Verbs:**
    Directions: Write the 23 helping verbs.

1. *D's*   a. _____   b. _____   c. _____

2. *H's*   a. _____   b. _____   c. _____

3. *M's*   a. _____   b. _____   c. _____

4. *Ould's* a. _____   b. _____   c. _____

5. *To be:* a. _____   c. _____   e. _____   g. _____

            b. _____   d. _____   f. _____   h. _____

6. *Others:* a. _____   b. _____   c. _____
        ༀༀༀༀༀༀༀༀༀༀༀༀ

H. **Irregular Verbs:**
    Directions: Underline the subject once and the correct verb phrase twice.

1. I had (taken, took) extra socks along.

2. Chan should have (drove, driven).

3. You must have (ran, run) fast.

4. Juan could have (went, gone) home.

5. Dad may have (drank, drunk) the milk.

6. Has she (swum, swam) the English Channel?

I.   **Subjects, Verbs, and Direct Objects:**
Directions: Cross out any prepositional phrases. Underline the subject once and the verb/verb phrase twice. Label any direct object – **D.O.**

1.   A child without a partner for the game grabbed my hand.

2.   Do you make your campsite by a stream?

෨෨෨෨෨෨෨෨෨෨෨෨෨

J.   **Sit/Set, Lie/Lay, and Rise/Raise:**
Directions: Delete any prepositional phrases. Underline the subject once and the verb/verb phrase twice. Label any direct object – **D.O.**

1.   Lily (sits, sets) her books under this shelf.   3.   They (rise, raise) early.

2.   Your pants are (lying, laying) here.   4.   (Lie, Lay) still.

෨෨෨෨෨෨෨෨෨෨෨෨෨

K.   **Tenses:**
Directions: Underline the subject once and the verb or verb phrase twice. Write the tense (*present, past,* or *future*) in the blank.

1.   _____ I shall bring my horse.

2.   _____ Sammy collects paperweights.

3.   _____ A hostess greeted her guests.

෨෨෨෨෨෨෨෨෨෨෨෨෨

L.   **Linking Verbs:**
Directions: Write the 20 linking verbs.

1. (to) _l____   5. (to) _a____   9. (to) _s____   13. _i__   17. _w___

2. (to) _f____   6. (to) _b____   10. (to) _s____   14. _a__   18. _b___

3. (to) _t____   7. (to) _g____   11. (to) _s____   15. _a__   19. _b___

4. (to) _s____   8. (to) _r____   12. (to) _b____   16. _w__   20. _b___

196

M. Action Verb or Linking Verb?:
   Directions: Place **X** if the verb is linking.

1. _____ The breeze **feels** good.   3. _____ Clover **grew** in the field.

2. _____ I **feel** sandpaper for texture.   4. _____ Her face **grew** red.

ৰৰৰৰৰৰৰৰৰৰৰৰ

N. Infinitives:
1. Write an infinitive: _____

ৰৰৰৰৰৰৰৰৰৰৰৰ

O. Transitive and Intransitive Verbs:
   Directions: Underline the subject once and the verb or verb phrase twice.
              Label any direct object - **D.O.** Write **T** if the verb is transitive;
              write **I** if the verb is intransitive.
   Remember: **A transitive verb will have a direct object.**
              D.O.T. > Direct Object = Transitive

1. _____ She soaked her feet.   3. _____ We installed a deadbolt.

2. _____ Bob closed the blinds.   4. _____ These ladybugs are big.

ৰৰৰৰৰৰৰৰৰৰৰৰ

P. Abstract and Concrete Nouns:
   Directions: Place a ✓ if the noun is abstract.
1. ___ calendar   3. ___ glee

2. ___ worm   4. ___ dizziness

ৰৰৰৰৰৰৰৰৰৰৰৰ

Q. Singular and Plural Nouns:
   Directions: Write the correct spelling of each plural noun.

1. facility - _____   6. channel - _____

2. service - _____   7. convoy - _____

3. hello - _____   8. child - _____

4. bonus - _____   9. arch - _____

5. belief - _____   10. series - _____

R. **Possessive Nouns:**
    Directions: Write the possessive and the item(s) owned in each blank.

1. moss on that tree - _____

2. eggs of penguins - _____

3. lace on a dress - _____

ॐॐॐॐॐॐॐॐॐॐॐॐ

S. **Nouns Used as Subjects, Direct Objects, and Indirect Objects:**
    Directions: Label any subject (**S.**), direct object (**D.O.**), and indirect object (**I.O.**).

1. Levi lost his baseball card.

2. Kim handed Jasmine a ticket.

ॐॐॐॐॐॐॐॐॐॐॐॐ

T. **Predicate Nominatives:**
    Directions: Underline the subject once and the verb twice. Label a
                  predicate nominative – **P.N.** Write the inverted form in the blank.
**Remember: A predicate nominative occurs <u>after</u> a linking verb and means the same as
              the subject.**

1. My father was the manager of that hockey team.

    _____

2. Ginger is one spice with a yellowish color.

    _____

ॐॐॐॐॐॐॐॐॐॐॐॐ

U. **Identifying Nouns:**
    Directions: Circle any nouns.
Remember: Determiners will help you to find some nouns.

1. A bag of potato chips lay on their kitchen sink.

2. John's friend gave his cousin several golf balls and an old club.

V. Descriptive Adjectives:

Directions: Write a descriptive adjective in each blank. Draw an arrow from the descriptive adjective to the noun it modifies (goes over to).

1. That _____ blanket needs to be washed.

2. Is _____ food delicious?

3. Loni's family used a _____ cart to carry their packages.

🙘🙘🙘🙘🙘🙘🙘🙘🙘🙘🙘

W.   Limiting (Determining) Adjectives:

- ❑ **Articles: a, an, the**
- ❑ **Demonstratives: this, that, these, those**
- ❑ **Possessive Pronouns: my, his, her, your, its, our, their, whose**
- ❑ **Numbers:** Example: *fifty-two* cards
- ❑ **Indefinites: any, few, no, many, most, several, some**
- ❑ **Possessive Nouns:** Example: a *pig's* snout

Directions: Write an appropriate limiting adjective from each category.

1. **Article** – _____ drink is cold.   4. **Possessive pronouns** – _____ drink is cold.

2. **Demonstratives** – _____ drinks are cold.   5. **Possessive nouns** – _____ drink is cold.

3. **Numbers** – _____ drinks are cold.   6. **Indefinites** – _____ drinks are cold.

🙘🙘🙘🙘🙘🙘🙘🙘🙘🙘🙘

X. Limiting Adjectives:

Remember: Some words can be limiting adjectives if they modify a noun. That same word will not be a limiting adjective if it stands alone.

Examples: I need **one** dollar   Adjective – *one* dollar

May I have ***one***?   *One* what? We don't know. *One* is not an adjective.

Directions: Place a ✓ in the blank if the boldfaced word is a limiting (determining) adjective. If the word is an adjective, write the boldfaced word and the noun that it modifies (goes over to) in the wide blank.

1. ___   **Many** castles were built in 1500. _____

2. ___   Do you want **this** balloon? _____

3. ___   Do you want **this**? _____

Y. **Proper Adjectives:**
> **A proper adjective is a descriptive word based on a proper noun.**

> **Mexico (noun)**   the **M**exican hat *dance*

Directions: Circle the proper adjective. Draw an arrow to the word it modifies.

1. I like your Canadian accent.

2. The French perfume smells good.

3. Do you like Siamese cats?

4. Jo climbed a Rocky Mountain slope.

ॐॐॐॐॐॐॐॐॐॐॐॐॐ

Z. **Predicate Adjectives:**
> *Sometimes an adjective occurs after the verb but describes the subject.*
> *This is called a predicate adjective.*
>
> Directions: Cross out any prepositional phrases. Underline the subject once
> and the verb twice. Label the predicate adjective – **P.A.**

1. Our watering can looks new.

2. His hat is wide and floppy.

3. This soda tastes flat.

4. The table's edge seems sharp.

ॐॐॐॐॐॐॐॐॐॐॐॐॐ

AA. **Degrees of Adjectives:**
> Directions: Circle the correct answer.

1. Your voice is (deeper, deepest) than mine.

2. My scalp is (more tender, tenderer) than the skin on my hands.

3. Mocha is the (more active, most active) kitten of the entire litter.

4. Thomas Jefferson was one of the (more educated, most educated)
people in the colonies.

ॐॐॐॐॐॐॐॐॐॐॐॐॐ

BB. **Identifying Adjectives:**
> Directions: Circle any adjectives.

1. Dad made two pitchers of fresh, sweet lemonade for the afternoon picnic.

2. Val asked a few questions about large, fast-running ostriches.

200

PERSONAL PRONOUNS:

Pronouns take the place of NOUNS. <u>Sally</u> likes berries.

<u>She</u> likes berries.

She (pronoun) takes the place of *Sally* (noun).

Pronouns agree in number and gender.

Number: Two comics told **their** jokes. (*Two* requires ***their.***)

Gender (male or female):   A princess walked to **her** car.

(Use a female pronoun [she, her] with a girl or a woman. Use a male pronoun [he, him] with a boy or man.)

Note: If you aren't sure if the noun is female or male, you may use his/her.
         However, *his* has become acceptable in this situation.

Nominative Pronouns (also called Subjective Pronouns)	**Objective Pronouns**	**Possessive Pronouns**
I	me	my, mine
he	him	his
she	her	her, hers
you	you	your, yours
it	it	its
we	us	our, ours
they	them	their, theirs
who	whom	whose
Use in a sentence:	**Use in a sentence:**	**Use in a sentence:**
1. Subject	1. Object of a Preposition	Shows Ownership
2. Predicate Nominatives	2. Direct Object	
	3. Indirect Object	

✧

Nominative Pronouns: **I, he, she, you, it, we, they, who**

A nominative pronoun can serve as a **subject** or a **predicate nominative**.

Subject:

You have learned that a subject of a sentence tells the *who* or *what* of a sentence.

The **boy** rode a skateboard.   The subject of the sentence is *boy*.

He rode a skateboard.   The subject is *he*.

Look at the ° above. *He* is on the list of nominative pronouns.

Nominative pronouns are also called **subjective** pronouns.

෨෨෨෨෨෨෨෨෨෨෨෨෨෨෨෨෨෨෨

Directions: Insert a nominative pronoun for the boldfaced noun or nouns.

1. **Jake** delivers pizza in the evening.   _____ delivers pizza in the evening.

2. **Lana** and **her brother** hike in the Smokey Mountains.   _____ hike in the Smoky Mountains.

3. **Bo** and (your name)_____ look at pictures. Bo and _____ look at pictures.

4. That **bear** is huge. _____ is huge.

5. **Levi and** (your name)_____ eat ketchup on fries.   _____ eat ketchup on fries.

6. Which **person** needs a ride? _____ needs a ride?

7. His **mother** is the woman with red hair. _____ is the woman with red hair.

8. (Your friend's name) _____, do _____ want a drink?

☼

Nominative Pronouns: **I, he, she, you, it, we, they, who**

A nominative pronoun can serve as a subject or a **predicate nominative**.

Predicate Nominative:

You have learned that a predicate nominative occurs after a (linking) verb and means the same as the subject.

Their dad is the **surfer** with black hair.

P.N.
Their <u>dad</u> <u>is</u> the **surfer** ~~with black hair~~.

Invert the sentence to offer a proof.

Proof: <u>The surfer (with black hair) is their dad</u>.

☼To replace *surfer* with a pronoun is tricky. First, the pronoun has to be on the nominative pronoun list: **I, he, she, you, it, we, they,** and **who**.

Their dad is the **surfer** with black hair.

Could we use *him*?   Their dad is that surfer (him) with gray hair. No! *Him* is not on the nominative pronoun list. We must use **he**! **He** is on the list of nominative pronouns.

Their dad is **he** ~~with black hair~~.

Proof: <u>He is their dad</u>.
ॐॐॐॐॐॐॐॐॐ

Directions: Circle the correct pronoun. Write the proof on the line.

1. The winners were (us, we).   Proof: _____

2. Her dad is (him, he) ~~in a suit~~.   Proof: _____

3. The champs are (they, them). Proof: _____

4. My friend is (she, her) ~~with bangs~~.   Proof: _____

5. The first person in line was (me, I).   Proof: _____

PRONOUNS

Subjects
Predicate Nominatives

Nominative Pronouns: **I, he, she, you, it, we, they, who**

A nominative pronoun can serve as a **subject** or a **predicate nominative**.

ન૭ન૭ન૭ન૭ન૭ન૭ન૭ન૭ન૭ન૭ન૭ન૭ન૭ન૭ન૭ન૭

A.   Directions: Delete any prepositional phrases. Underline the subject once and
the verb twice. In the blank, replace the subject with a nominative
pronoun and write the verb with it.

Example: A <u>bug</u> <u>flew</u> ~~around our tent~~.

_____It flew._____

1.   A fisherman cast his line.

_____

2.   Several café owners met.

_____

3.   My friends and I played at a park.

_____

ન૭ન૭ન૭ન૭ન૭ન૭ન૭ન૭ન૭ન૭

B.   Directions: Delete any prepositional phrases. Underline the subject once and
the verb twice. Write **P.N.** above the predicate nominative.
Write the proof.

1.   The senator is she with the briefcase.

Proof: _____

2.   The first person through the door was I.

Proof: _____

3.   His brothers-in-law are they in polo shirts.

Proof: _____

4.   Your uncle is who?

Proof: _____

Objective Pronouns: **me, him, her, you, it, us, them, whom**
Objective pronouns can serve as an *object* of a preposition, a direct *object*, or an **indirect *object*.**

Remember that an object of a preposition is a noun or pronoun that ends a prepositional phrase.

O.P.
Lean against **me**.   prepositional phrase ~ *against me*

object of the preposition = *me*. **Me** is an objective pronoun.

A.   Directions: Circle the prepositional phrase.

1.   Sit beside us.

2.   Hannah went with him.

3.   With whom are you going?

Remember that a direct object receives the action of a verb.

D.O.
A bug bit **her**.   **Her** is a direct object. **Her** is an objective pronoun.

B.   Directions: Underline the subject once and the verb twice. Label the direct
                     object – **D.O.**

1.   A paper airplane hit me.   3.   Their sister joined her.

2.   I enjoyed it!   4.   Mrs. Crabb called them.

**Remember that an indirect object is a noun or pronoun that indirectly receives the action
of a verb. You can put *to* or *for* in front of an indirect object.**

I.O.   D.O.
My niece drew us a picture.   **Us** is an indirect object.

C.   Directions: Underline the subject once and the verb/verb phrase twice. Label
                     the direct object – **D.O.** and the indirect object – **I. O.**

1.   He handed me a tall, striped cup.

2.   A shoe shiner handed us his card.

3.   Tara gave them her apology.

An objective pronoun can serve as an *object* of a preposition, a **direct object**, or an **indirect object**. (me, him, her, you, it, us, them, whom)

A.   Directions: Tell if the boldfaced pronoun serves as a direct object (**D.O.**), indirect object (**I.O.**), or an object of the preposition (**O.P.**).

1.   _____   I like **you**.

2.   _____   Ken handed **us** a pen.

3.   _____   Stop **them**!

4.   _____   There is a wasp near **you**.

5.   _____   Gretta greeted **me**.

6.   _____   The grocer handed **him** a sack of oranges.

7.   _____   The wind is blowing; walk against **it**.

8.   _____   For **whom** are you waiting?

～～～～～～～～～～～～～～～～～～～～～～～～～～～～～～～～

A nominative pronoun can serve as a **subject** or as a **predicate nominative.**
I, he, she, you, it, we, they, who

A.   Directions: Tell if the boldfaced pronoun serves as a subject - **S.** or a predicate nominative - **P.N.**

1.   _____   **You** have a scar on your arm.

2.   _____   Along the way, **we** dropped crumbs for the ducks.

3.   _____   Are **they** finished with their project?

4.   _____   His first neighbor is **she** in the blue dress.

5.   _____   Their choice was **I**.

6.   _____   Mario, Dana, Jana, Tate, and **he** met at a pizza parlor.

206

Directions: Circle the correct pronoun. **(The boldfaced information tells how the pronoun functions.)**

1.   Come with (I, me).   **– object of the preposition**

2.   A puppy licked (us, we).   **– direct object**

3.   (I, me) enjoy scuba diving.   **– subject**

4.   Micah handed (they, them) towels.   **– indirect object**

5.   The last person to enter the room was (him, he).   **– predicate nominative**

6.   Take (I, me) with you.   **– direct object**

7.   To (whom, who) did you send that email?   **– object of the preposition**

8.   A jogger ran by (her, she).   **– object of the preposition**

9.   A safety expert handed (he, him) an orange cone.   **– indirect object**

10.   Glenda and (her, she) agree.   **– subject**

11.   The symphony leader chose (them, they) to help.   **– direct object**

12.   A tornado passed near (us, we).   **– object of the preposition**

13.   May Jamil and (we, us) stand here?   **– subject**

14.   Mom baked (they, them) cookies for a bake sale.   **– indirect object**

15.   That matter does not concern (I, me).   **– direct object**

16.   His dad is (he, him) in the red tie.   **– predicate nominative**

17.   (Who, Whom) has a good idea?   **– subject**

Compound means more than one. To make a decision about pronoun usage in compounds, think about <u>how</u> the pronoun is used in the sentence.

If the pronoun serves as a subject or predicate nominative, use *I, he, she, we, they,* or *who.*

If the pronoun serves as a direct object, indirect object, or object of the preposition, use *me, him, her, us, them,* or *whom.*

FINGER TRICK: **If you are unsure, try placing your finger over the first part of the compound. Then make the decision.**

Example: John and (I, me) want to attend a boxing match.
---------- (**I**, me) want to attend a boxing match.

Place finger here.

∂∂∂∂∂∂∂∂∂∂∂∂∂∂∂∂∂∂∂∂∂

Directions: Circle the correct pronoun.

1. Joe and (we, us) went to the dentist.

2. My friend and (I, me) will wax the floor.

3. The X-ray person gave Josh and (they, them) several films.

4. Please sit beside Tate and (us, we).

5. The clerk handed Marta and (her, she) some change.

6. Do you want to go with my brother and (I, me)?

7. Our cousins are Dirk and (he, him).

8. Many students and (them, they) went to a pep rally.

9. The coach presented her teammates and (her, she) a trophy.

10. Don't put Jake and (him, he) in the first row.

11. A shoe-repair lady and (him, he) will put new heels on our shoes.

12. Please give your parents and (we, us) your answer.

Reflexive pronouns end with **self** or **selves.** Reflexive pronouns are <u>myself</u>, <u>himself</u>, <u>herself</u>, <u>itself</u>, <u>yourself</u>, <u>ourselves</u>, and <u>themselves</u>. A reflexive pronoun reflects back to another noun or pronoun in a sentence. The word to which a reflexive pronoun refers back is called an ***antecedent.***

        Examples: Taylor did the whole job by herself.
                The antecedent is **Taylor.** *Herself* refers back to **Taylor.**

                 A cat licked itself.
                The antecedent is **cat.** *Itself* refers back to **cat.**

DO NOT USE hisself or theirselves. They are incorrect.

Directions: Circle the reflexive pronoun. Write the antecedent in the blank after the sentence.

    Remember: The word to which a reflexive pronoun refers back is called an ***antecedent.***

1.   Josh checked the equipment **himself.**   _____

2.   I want to do the project by **myself.**   _____

3.   You must do it **yourself.**   _____

4.   The guests helped **themselves** to food. _____

5.   A kitten looked at **itself** in a mirror.   _____

6.   Julie painted the entire scene **herself.**   _____

7.   Bo and I will make pizza **ourselves.**   _____

8.   The sisters planned a trip **themselves.** _____

9.   Toni, **herself,** was not hurt.   _____

10. Do you want to sit by **yourself**?   _____

The demonstrative pronouns are **this, that, these, those.**

Examples: I want **this**.   Do you want **these**?
              That is my favorite!   **Those** are yours.

This and **that** are singular. **These** and **those** are plural and refer to two or more.

Them is not a demonstrative pronoun.

Incorrect: Them is for sale.   Correct: Those are for sale.

If *this, that, those,* or *these* modify (go over to) another word, they function as adjectives, not pronouns.

Examples: This is old.   (pronoun)
              This bucket is old.   (adjective – *this bucket.*)

ઠ~ઠ~ઠ~ઠ~ઠ~ઠ~ઠ~ઠ~ઠ~ઠ~ઠ~ઠ~ઠ~

Directions: Write **P** if the boldfaced word serves as a pronoun. Write **A** if the
              boldfaced word serves as an adjective and draw an arrow to the
              noun it modifies (goes over to).

1. _____   **This** is awful.

2. _____   Do you want **these** potato skins?

3. _____   We put **that** towel in the hamper.

4. _____   I believe that **those** are mine.

5. _____   I can't believe **that**.

6. _____   Is **this** bag heavy?

7. _____   Put more salt on **this**, please.

8. _____   Who brought **these** to the classroom?

9. _____   I need to remove **this** gum from my shirt.

10. _____   **These** rugs must be cleaned.

210

Interrogative pronouns ask questions.
The interrogative pronouns are **who**, **whom**, **whose**, **which**, and **what**.

Whose, *which*, and *what* are pronouns when they stand alone.

Examples: **Whose** is this?
Which do you want?
What do you know about the flight?

Whose, *which*, and *what* are adjectives when they modify another word.

Examples: **Whose** coat is on the floor? (**Whose** *coat*)
Have you decided **which** pattern you like? (**which** *pattern*)
What answer do you expect? (**What** *answer*)

ର୍ଜ୍ଜ୍ଜ୍ଜ୍ଜ୍ଜ୍ଜ୍ଜ୍ଜ୍ଜ୍ଜ୍ଜ୍

Directions: Write **P** if the boldfaced word serves as a pronoun. Write **A** if the boldfaced word serves as an adjective and draw an arrow to the noun it modifies (goes over to).

1. _____ **What** is the answer?

2. _____ Do you know **which** apartment is his?

3. _____ **Whose** might be chosen?

4. _____ **What** fern is this?

5. _____ **Which** do you need?

6. _____ **Whose** car is in the driveway?

7. _____ I don't know **which** is the best.

8. _____ Have you determined **which** flight is leaving?

9. _____ **What** did you say?

10. _____ Are you aware **which** story is mine?

211

Indefinite pronouns take the place of nouns.
Indefinite pronouns include **anyone**, **everybody**, **everyone**, **nobody**, **none**, **somebody**, and **someone**.

Examples: Has **anyone** seen my notebook?
              She has **none**.

Indefinite pronouns also include **any**, **both**, **each**, **either**, **few**, **many**, **neither**, and **no**. When these words stand alone, they are pronouns. However, they are adjectives when they modify another word.

Examples: **Both** are going.   (*Both* is a pronoun here; it stands alone.)
              Both girls are going.   (*Both* is an adjective here; *both* girls.)

              I don't like **either**.   (*Either* is a pronoun here; it stands alone.)
              I don't like **either** CD.   (*Either* is an adjective here; *either* CD.)

ช่ช่ช่ช่ช่ช่ช่ช่ช่ช่ช่ช่ช่

A.   Directions: Write an indefinite pronoun that makes sense in each blank.

1.   Did _____ buy milk?

2.   _____ left the top off the peanut butter.

3.   Sarah asked _____ to vote for her.

4.   _____ wants to know.

B.   Directions: Write **P** if the boldfaced word serves as a pronoun. Write **A** if the boldfaced word serves as an adjective and draw an arrow to the noun it modifies (goes over to).

1.   _____   **Some** helped.

2.   _____   He had hoped for **some** rain.

3.   _____   Do you want **any**?

4.   _____   Does she have **any** horses?

5.   _____   Chan bought **several** for his bike.

6.   _____   During the storm, **several** trees had fallen.

212

POSSESSIVE PRONOUNS

The possessive pronouns are:

my, mine
his
her, hers
your, yours
its
our, ours
their, theirs
whose

My, his, her, your, its, our, their, and *whose* are placed before nouns or other pronouns.

Examples: **my** cart   **her** name   **its** beak   **their** flight

his hats   **your** dad   **our** desks   **whose** bat

Mine, hers, yours, ours, and *theirs* are not placed before nouns or other pronouns (usually). They refer back to a noun or a pronoun in a sentence.

Examples: This drawing is **mine**.

That suitcase with the checked lining is **hers**.

The gift is **yours** to keep.

One of the cars is **ours**.

Is the puppy **theirs**?

Do you see that you can write possessive pronouns in two ways?

My cat is gray and white.   The gray and white cat is **mine**.

●Note that *his* does not change.

His cat is black.   The black cat is **his**.

●Notice that *its* does not have an apostrophe (’).

The possessive pronouns are **my**, **mine**, **his**, **her**, **hers**, **your**, **yours**, **its**, **our**, **ours**, **their**, **theirs**, and **whose**.

Examples: **my** friend   **her** lips   **its** paw   **their** parents
           his brother   **your** lungs   **our** trip   **whose** truck

Mine, hers, yours, ours, and *theirs* go to a noun or pronoun earlier in the sentence.

Examples: I think that those *raisins* are **mine**.
            Is that *marker* **hers**?
            Are these *blueprints* **yours**?
            That *motorcycle* is **ours**.
            Are these *baskets* **theirs**?

You can write most possessive pronouns in two ways:

Our house is yellow.   The yellow house is **ours**.

భేళేళేళేళేళేళేళేళేళేళేళే

Directions: Write a possessive pronoun that makes sense in each blank.

1. _____ friends agree with you.

2. Are _____ shoes new?

3. Marta and Lee rushed toward _____ mom.

4. _____ score was high.

5. Does _____ toe look bruised?

6. Before lunch, the librarian talked with _____ helpers.

7. Hans called, but _____ message was not clear.

8. A kangaroo hopped near _____ mother.

9. Has anyone seen _____ backpack?

10. _____ sandwich is this?

Its, **their**, and **your** are possessive pronouns. They are **not** spelled with an apostrophe ('). They modify (go over to) a noun or another pronoun.

> A cub snuggled next to **its** momma.   (**its** momma)
> They like **their** new apartment.   (**their** apartment)
> Is **your** chain new?   (**your** chain)

It's, **they're**, and **you're** are contractions. They use an apostrophe (').

> it's = it is   **It's** sunny today.
> they're = they are   **They're** eating strawberries on their cereal.
> you're = you are   I know that **you're** excited about the fair.

Directions: Circle the correct word.

1. What is (your, you're) address?

2. (Their, They're) waiting until the rain stops.

3. (Its, It's) time for lunch.

4. Are (your, you're) computer skills good?

5. (Their, They're) moving boxes are wet.

6. A prairie dog ran into (its, it's) hole.

7. My dad and (your, you're) grandfather are golfing.

8. Have you seen (they're, their) video game?

9. My fishing pole has tangled line and (its, it's) pole is bent.

10. In the late afternoon, (you're, your) expected to cut the grass.

11. (Their, They're) always in a hurry.

12. (It's, Its) not polite to burp at (your, you're) dinner table.

Possessive pronouns are **my, mine, his, her, hers, your, yours, its, our, ours, their, theirs**, and **whose**.

Possessive pronouns reflect back to another noun or pronoun in a sentence. The word to which a possessive pronoun refers back is called an ***antecedent***.

Example: Bill sent **his** cousin a yoyo.
(**Bill's**)

His refers back to Bill. ***Bill*** is the <u>antecedent</u> of *his*.

~ **You wouldn't use** *her*; **in this case, Bill is a boy.**

Example: Manny and Susan went to **their** karate class.
(**Manny and Susan's**)

Their refers back to Manny and Susan. ***Manny and Susan*** is the <u>antecedent</u> of *their*.

~ **You wouldn't use** *his* **or** *her*; **you are referring to both Manny and Susan.**

This is what is meant when the rule says that the possessive pronoun must agree in gender (boy-girl) and number with the antecedent.

≈≈≈≈≈≈≈≈≈≈≈≈≈≈≈≈≈≈≈≈≈

Directions: Circle the possessive pronoun. Write the antecedent in the blank after the sentence.

Remember: The word to which a possessive pronoun refers back is called an ***antecedent***.

1. Jake likes his new teacher.   _____

2. The teachers met in their office.   _____

3. That printer gave her bid at once.   _____

4. I like my watch.   _____

5. Someone left his sunglasses.   _____

6. Tyler and Loni want their lunch.   _____

7. A monkey scratched its arm.   _____

8. Jenny and I cleaned for our mother. _____
216

A. Nominative Pronouns:

Remember: Nominative pronouns can serve as a subject or a predicate nominative.
I, he, she, it, you, we, they, who

Directions: Write **S.** if the boldfaced pronoun serves as a subject; write **P.N.** if the boldfaced pronoun serves as a predicate nominative.

1. _____ Throughout the evening, **they** watched television.

2. _____ The chief engineer is **she** with the hard hat.

3. _____ During the last quarter of the game, **we** decided to leave.

4. _____ One winner of the funny car race was **he** in the blue car.

B. Objective Pronouns:

Remember: Objective pronouns can serve as a direct object, an indirect object, or an object of a preposition.
me, him, her, it, you, us, them, whom

Directions: Write **D.O.** if the boldfaced pronoun serves as a direct object, write **I.O** if the boldfaced pronoun serves as an indirect object, and write **O.P.** if the boldfaced pronoun serves as an object of the preposition.

1. _____ Her elbow jabbed **me** in the side.

2. _____ Go without **us**, please.

3. _____ Don't give **them** any more peanuts.

4. _____ Paula baked **him** wheat bread.

5. _____ Marco fielded the ball and threw **it** to first base.

6. _____ To **whom** did you give your note?

217

C. Pronoun Usage:

Directions: Circle the correct pronoun.

1.   (I, Me) have dug a hole for a bush.

2.   Did you receive a letter from (we, us)?

3.   Give (them, they) your name.

4.   The first to arrive at the party was (her, she).

5.   To (whom, who) are you sending this box?

6.   (He, Him) is studying Spanish.

7.   Hans wants to do the job (himself, hisself).

8.   A tray of muffins was placed between (us, we).

ฅ‑ฅ‑ฅ‑ฅ‑ฅ‑ฅ‑ฅ‑ฅ‑ฅ‑ฅ‑ฅ‑ฅ‑ฅ‑ฅ‑ฅ‑ฅ

D. Compound Pronoun Usage:

Reminder: Don't forget the finger trick.

Directions: Circle the correct pronoun.

1.   Would you like to come with Deka and (me, I)?

2.   The janitor, the window washer, and (him, he) met for a meeting.

3.   Gabe and (us, we) need to redo our homework.

4.   The president of her company and (her, she) discussed her new job.

5.   Pass Grammy and (them, they) the mashed potatoes.

6.   The winners of the game were Sid and (I, me).

E. Reflexive Pronouns:

Directions: Write six reflexive pronouns.

1. _____   4. _____

2. _____   5. _____

3. _____   6. _____

কচকচকচকচকচকচকচকচকচকচকচ

F. Pronoun or Adjective?:

Directions: Place **PRO.** in the blank if the boldfaced word serves as a pronoun.

1. _____   Did you find **that**?

2. _____   **Which** knob is copper?

3. _____   **Both** boys laughed and waved to us.

4. _____   After basketball practice, **some** stayed to shoot hoops.

5. _____   Put **these** stickers on your book cover.

6. _____   **Many** of the band members march in every parade.

কচকচকচকচকচকচকচকচকচকচকচ

G. Indefinite Pronouns:

Directions: Write an indefinite pronoun that makes sense in each blank.

1. Did _____ hear that?

2. The announcer asked _____ to stand.

3. _____ answered the telephone.

H. Possessive Pronouns:

Directions: Unscramble these possessive pronouns.

1. s h i - _____   6. t e r i h - _____

2. y m - _____   7. u r o - _____

3. s r h e - _____   8. u y r o - _____

4. r u o s y - _____   9. e n i m - _____

5. s t i - _____   10. o s h e w - _____

I. Possessive Pronoun Usage:

Directions: Circle the correct pronoun.

1. Mr. Jones carried a cane and (his, her) own luggage.

2. I like (them, their) scooters.

3. The guides showed (his, their) groups through the museum.

4. Carrie likes the dog that she bought; it is (her, hers).

J. Antecedents:

Directions: Circle the possessive pronoun; write its antecedent in the blank.

1. _____   Some children brought their marbles to the playground.

2. _____   Mary lifted her baton and began.

3. _____   Did Mario and Jan lead their team to victory?

4. _____   We must use our talents to solve this puzzle.

220

A. **Subject/Verb:**
   Directions: Cross out any prepositional phrases. Underline the subject once
              and the verb or verb phrase twice. Place any infinitive in
              parentheses **( )**. Label any direct object – **D.O.**

1. Three horses from a local farm will enter a horserace near Portland.

2. Within an hour of her father's call, Mom left for the airport.

3. One of the singers stepped behind a microphone to sing a solo.

4. Rustic logs are lying behind their office building at a small airport.

5. Before lunch or dinner, ranchers wash and dry their hands at an outdoor sink.

                              ✿ ✿ ✿

B. **Compound Subjects and Verbs:**
   Directions: Cross out any prepositional phrases. Underline the subject once
              and the verb or verb phrase twice.

1. A chef and his assistant stirred sauce into the noodles.

2. During a pep rally, girls and boys sang songs and cheered for their team.

3. The newsman and the weather reporter talked about a tornado in the area.

4. Move that purple sofa here but keep the pillows on it.

                              ✿ ✿ ✿

C. **Subject-Verb Agreement:**
   Directions: Delete any prepositional phrases. Underline the subject once.
              Underline the verb that agrees with the subject twice.

1. Ms. Link (works, work) near a bus station.

2. Your shirt with blue buttons (are, is) beside the white one.

3. One of the buses (arrive, arrives) at noon.

4. Their father and mother (grow, grows) herbs for cooking.

D. **Contractions:**
   Directions: Write the contraction.

1. did not - _____   5. I am - _____   9. do not - _____

2. he is - _____   6. who is - _____   10. I have - _____

3. cannot - _____   7. they have - _____   11. they are - _____

4. we are - _____   8. will not - _____   12. would not - _____

᪥᪥᪥

E. **You're/Your, It's/Its, and They're/Their/There:**
   Directions: Circle the correct word.

1. Is (there, their, they're) a problem?

2. I want (you're, your) help.

3. If (its, it's) raining, let's use (there, their, they're) umbrella.

᪥᪥᪥

F. **Irregular Verbs:**
   Directions: Underline the subject once and the correct verb phrase twice.

1. Has Tara (brung, brought) some water?

2. Cal must have (spoke, spoken) early.

3. I should have (ran, run) further.

4. Hannah might have (come, came) alone.

5. Have your new pigs (ate, eaten) anything?

6. The painter must have (fallen, fell).

7. That stable boy has (went, gone) home.

8. This hose may have (sprang, sprung) a leak.

9. You should have (drunk, drank) more juice.

222

G. **Sit/Set, Lie/Lay, and Rise/Raise:**

   Directions: Delete any prepositional phrases. Underline the subject once
   and the verb/verb phrase twice. Label any direct object – **D.O.**

1. We had been (lying, laying) near a fire.   3.   Mia (rises, raises) ostriches.

2. Are they (setting, sitting) with Stan?   4.   (Lie, Lay) here.

   ❧ ❧ ❧

H. **Tenses:**

   Directions: Underline the subject once and the verb or verb phrase
   twice. Write the tense (*present, past,* or *future*) in the blank.

1. _____ His puppy yelps constantly.

2. _____ Chan and Janie enjoy chess.

3. _____ Fireworks shot into the air.

4. _____ Marta asked me to stay.

5. _____ Toby will join the Army soon.

   ❧ ❧ ❧

I. **Action Verb or Linking Verb?:**

   Directions: Place **X** if the verb is linking.

1. _____ This oatmeal **smells** good.   3.   _____ My bare toes **are** dirty.

2. _____ Tate **appeared** breathless.   4.   _____ She **remained** in her seat.

   ❧ ❧ ❧

J. **Transitive and Intransitive Verbs:**

   Directions: Place a ✓ if the verb is transitive.

   Remember: A transitive verb will have a direct object.
   D.O.T. > Direct **O**bject = **T**ransitive

1. _____ Lu stood up.   3.   _____ Do you like mysteries?

2. _____ We planted apple trees.   4.   _____ One camel spit at me.

223

K. **Abstract and Concrete Nouns:**

   Directions: Place a ✓ if the noun is abstract.

1. ____   love   3. ____   harm   5. ____   hubcap

2. ____   kindness   4. ____   pin   6. ____   grace

&&&

L. **Common and Proper Nouns:**

   Directions: Place a ✓ if the noun is proper.

1. ____   MOUNTAIN   3. ____   ELBOW   5. ____   BANKER

2. ____   TENNESSEE   4. ____   OZARKS   6. ____   CHINA

&&&

M. **Singular and Plural Nouns:**

   Directions: Write the correct spelling of each plural noun.

1. halo - _____   6. goose - _____

2. march - _____   7. touch - _____

3. charity - _____   8. railway - _____

4. airbus - _____   9. skiff - _____

5. penknife - _____   10. laughter - _____

&&&

N. **Nouns Used as Subjects, Direct Objects, Indirect Objects, and Objects of the Preposition:**

   Directions: Label any subject (**S.**), direct object (**D.O.**), indirect object (**I.O.**), and object of the preposition (**O.P.**).

1. We added milk to our sliced bananas.   3. Jack told us the truth.

2. I am searching a database.   4. Did you find a toad near our tent?

O. **Possessive Nouns:**

     Directions: Write the possessive and the item(s) owned in each blank.

1. carvings on a desk - _____

2. a check received by Ross - _____

3. bags carried by a traveler - _____

4. a moat belonging to a castle - _____

5. competition of more than one poodle - _____

6. dance class attended by more than one child - _____

ళళళ

P. **Predicate Nominatives:**

     Directions: Underline the subject once and the verb twice. Label a
                  predicate nominative – **P.N.** Write the inverted form in the blank.

1. A bay is an evergreen tree with laurel leaves.

    _____

2. That blizzard was our worst storm.

    _____

3. Nightingales are birds with a pretty song.

    _____

ళళళ

Q. **Identifying Nouns:**

     Directions: Circle any nouns.

Remember: Determiners will help you to find some nouns.

1. I bought two pints of milk, bread, several tomatoes, and bacon for my lunch.

2. The conductor on that train collects tickets from many passengers.

R. **Descriptive Adjectives:**

Directions: Write a descriptive adjective in each blank.

1. _____ deer   3. _____ tie

2. _____ plant   4. _____ snowboard

౷౷౷

S. **Proper Adjectives:**

Directions: Circle a proper adjective.   Underline any predicate adjectives.

1.   That African nation is powerful.

2.   Her hair was once red.

3.   Her brother is dating a British model.

౷౷౷

T. **Limiting (Determining) Adjectives:**

▌**Articles: a, an, the**
▌**Demonstratives: this, that, these, those**
▌**Possessive Pronouns: my, his, her, your, its, our, their, whose**
▌**Numbers:** Example: *one* sign
▌**Indefinites: any, few, no, many, most, several, some**
▌**Possessive Nouns:** Example: an *elephant's* trunk

Directions: Write an appropriate limiting adjective from each category.

1. Article – _____ house is old.   4. Possessive pronouns – _____ house is old.

2. Demonstratives – _____ houses are old.   5. Possessive nouns – _____ house is old.

3. Numbers – _____ houses are old.   6. Indefinites – _____ houses are old.

౷౷౷

U. **Identifying Adjectives:**

Directions: Circle any adjectives.

1.   Fifteen plates of spicy chicken wings were placed on a long, wooden table.

2.   Several reporters asked the thief about his female partner in a petty crime.

V. **Degrees of Adjectives:**

     Directions: Circle the correct answer.

1. This large peach is (jucier, juciest) than the small one.

2. His second fable was (more creative, creativer) than his first.

3. Micah is the (more curious, most curious) triplet.

4. Of all the lifeguards, Mickey was (more dependable, most dependable).

                    ☙☙☙

W. **Adverbs Telling *How, When, Where, and To What Extent*:**

Directions: Delete any prepositional phrases. Underline the subject once and the
                verb or verb phrase twice. Circle any adverbs that tells *how, when,
                where, or to what extent.*

1. Mom always reads that newsletter completely.

2. The toddler tends to stumble rather frequently.

3. Yesterday, some teachers went downtown after school.

4. Tessa sweeps quite quickly but well.

5. Later, they went down into the cellar and walked around.

                    ☙☙☙

X. **Degrees of Adverbs:**

     Directions: Circle the correct answer.

1. She checked her blood pressure (more carefully, most carefully) the third
    time.

2. Chessa skates (more easily, most easily) than her sister.

3. Fido jumps (higher, highest) of the five dogs.

4. The tall athlete shot (more accurately, most accurately) in the final game.

5. Of the two lions, the first paced (more restlessly, most restlessly).   227

Name_____

Date_____

The four types of sentences are declarative, interrogative, imperative, and exclamatory.

1. A **declarative** sentence makes a statement; it ends in a period (**.**).
   Example: His hair is black**.**

2. An **interrogative** sentence asks a question; it ends in a question mark (**?**).
   Example: Is Tom sick**?**

3. An **imperative** sentence gives a command; it ends in a period (**.**).
   Example: Tear this into pieces**.**

4. An **exclamatory** sentence shows emotion; it ends in an exclamation point (**!**).
   Example: Look out**!**

ह‍ह‍ह‍ह‍ह‍ह‍ह‍ह‍ह‍ह‍ह‍ह‍ह

A.   Directions: Write the sentence type on the line.

1. _____   Stop that car!

2. _____   Put a leash on your dog.

3. _____   This book has many pictures.

4. _____   Do you wear a helmet?

B.   Directions: Write the sentence type on the line. Place a period, question
                  mark, or exclamation point at the end of the sentence.

1. _____   Do you have a ruler

2. _____   Mafalde is a type of pasta

3. _____   Wow! We did it

4. _____   Go to recess

5. _____   We asked if we could stay

6. _____   Be sure to exit here

228

The four types of sentences are declarative, interrogative, imperative, and exclamatory.

1. A **declarative** sentence makes a statement; it ends in a period (**.**).

2. An **interrogative** sentence asks a question; it ends in a question mark (**?**).

3. An **imperative** sentence gives a command; it ends in a period (**.**).

4. An **exclamatory** sentence shows emotion; it ends in an exclamation point (**!**).

A. Directions: Write the type of sentence. Place a punctuation mark at the end of each sentence.

1. _____   Put putty in this hole

2. _____   This has a fruity flavor

3. _____   How do I make fondue

4. _____   Let's play checkers

5. _____   Divide your paper into two columns

6. _____   A buran is a type of storm

7. _____   Yikes! We're lost

B. Directions: Write the sentence type required.

1. declarative: _____

2. interrogative: _____

3. exclamatory: _____

4. imperative: _____

FRIENDLY LETTER

The parts of a friendly letter are the **heading**, the **salutation** (greeting), the **body**, the **closing**, and the **signature**.

A three-lined formal heading will be used. In informal letters, the date is frequently the only item included.

In a formal letter, as in all formal writing, abbreviations are not used. The exception to this is the postal code for states. A postal code is capitalized, and no punctuation is used.

Examples:	Vermont = VT	Missouri = MO
	North Dakota = ND	Idaho = ID

FRIENDLY LETTER PARTS:

		HOUSE NUMBER AND STREET NAME
		or POST OFFICE BOX
	HEADING	CITY, STATE ZIP CODE
		COMPLETE DATE (no abbreviations)

GREETING   Dear _____,

BODY   The message is written here. Indent at least five letters. You may skip a line between the greeting and the body. Maintain margins on both sides of the paper. Be sure to start a new paragraph each time you change topics.

CLOSING	Sincerely,
SIGNATURE	Writer's Name

~~~~~~

Important Notes:

A. Note the use of commas. Place a comma between the city and state in the heading. Place one after the greeting. Place one at the end of the closing. Do **NOT** place a comma between the state and zip code in the heading.

B. Note that the heading, the closing, and the signature are lined up. You should be able to draw a straight line down the page.

C. Capitalize only the **first word** of a closing. Be sure that you spell *sincerely* and *truly* correctly.

D. Space a letter down a page; don't clump it at the top half.

E. Maintain margins. Set up your heading so that your longest line does not flow into the margin area.

ENVELOPE

The envelope for a friendly letter usually is in **block form**. That means that each line begins exactly below the first letter in the line before it.

YOUR NAME
HOUSE NUMBER AND STREET ADDRESS   **RETURN ADDRESS**
CITY, STATE   ZIP CODE

PERSON TO WHOM YOU ARE SENDING LETTER
HOUSE NUMBER AND STREET ADDRESS
CITY, STATE   ZIP CODE

Sample:

Misty Storm   ************
10031 North 90th Lane   STAMP
Scottsdale, AZ   85258   ************

Mr. and Mrs. James Tuley
288222 NW Boones Ferry Road
Wilsonville, OR   97070

IMPORTANT NOTES:

1. In a formal envelope, abbreviations are not used.

2. A variation of the block style allows for indenting each line. If this is chosen, both the return address and the regular address must be indented.

Name_____   **FRIENDLY LETTERS/**

Date_____   **ENVELOPES**

Write a friendly letter to a friend. Label the parts of your friendly letter.

_____
_____
_____
_____
_____
_____
_____
_____
_____
_____
_____
_____
_____
_____
_____
_____
_____
_____
_____
_____
_____
_____

B. Directions: Write your return address; then, address the envelope to a friend.

_____
_____   **STAMP**
_____
_____

                              _____
                              _____
                              _____

An **interjection is a word or phrase that shows strong emotion.**

A *phrase* is just a group of words. It does **not** express a complete thought.

An interjection ends with an exclamation point (**!**).

Word: Yeah!

Phrase: Far out!

A **sentence** that expresses strong emotion is called an **exclamatory sentence.**

A sentence contains both a subject and verb; it expresses a complete thought.

Example: Look out!   (You) <u>Look</u> out!

This expresses a complete thought. It is an exclamatory sentence, **not** an interjection.

❧❧❧❧❧❧❧

A.   Directions: Circle any interjection.

1.   Yikes! I see a bear!

2.   The elderly hippie smiled and said, "Right on!"

3.   Ouch! That hurt!

4.   "Oh dear!" Grandma murmured.

5.   We're leaving now! Yeah!

B.   Directions: Write an appropriate interjection in the blank.

1.   _____ Be quiet!

2.   You're wet! _____

3.   I'm winning! _____

And, but, and ***or*** are called coordinating **conjunctions.** They **connect** two or more items.

> Mark **and** I played basketball.

> You **or** Will must finish this job.

> He skis, **but** he doesn't snowboard.

However, *but* is a preposition, not a conjunction, when it means *except.*

❧❧❧❧❧

A. Directions: Circle any coordinating conjunction in each sentence.

1. Please bring a water bottle or a canteen.

2. The salesman spoke with a customer but looked in another direction.

3. Her mouse pad and note box are bright pink leather.

4. One student didn't run and play but sat alone.

5. You may choose vanilla or chocolate but not strawberry.

B. Directions: Two coordinating conjunctions might fit in each blank. Write the first in the blank and the second in the parentheses.

1. Randy _____ (_____) his sister worked in the school carnival booth.

2. The man climbed the tower _____ (_____) became dizzy.

3. Lars, Peter, _____ (_____) Julian played football on Saturday.

C. Directions: Write a sentence using the indicated coordinating conjunction.

1. (or) _____

2. (and) _____

3. (but) _____

Sentences: A sentence expresses a **complete thought**.
This can also be called an **independent clause**.
A sentence begins with a **capital letter** and ends with a
punctuation mark.

Fragments: A fragment does **not** express a complete thought.

~ Sometimes, a subject is missing.   **Example:**   My likes to snowboard.

~ Sometimes, a verb is missing.   **Example:**   Jan, Sara, and Chan to snowboard.

~ Some fragments have neither subject nor verb.

Example: In a hurry on the way to the bus after school.

Do not confuse an imperative sentence with a fragment.

Example: Go.   This has the subject, (You) – you understood. (You) Go.

~&~&~&~&~&~&~&~&~&~&~&~&~

Directions: Read each fragment. Using the fragment, write a sentence.

1.   Your is torn. _____

2.   Next time. _____

3.   A purred at our feet. _____

4.   Old oak tree down. _____

5.   Grass in their yard. _____

6.   A photo album in the drawer. _____

_____

7.   Grease all over. _____

8.   The vineyard on the hill. _____

Sentences: A sentence expresses a **complete thought**. This can also be called an **independent clause**. A sentence begins with a **capital letter** and ends with a **punctuation mark**.

Run-Ons: A run-on may consist of two or more sentences run together.
            Example: This ring is silver my brother made it.

If two complete sentences are separated by a comma, it is still a run-on.

Example: This ring is silver, my brother made it.

A run-on may consist of a group of sentences combined with too many conjunctions (*and, but, or*).

   Example: Later, the girl did a crossword puzzle **and** ate popcorn **and** then watched a television show **but** didn't like it.

A.   Directions: Write **S** if the words form a sentence. Write **R-O** if the words form a run-on.

1. ____   Franny threw dice onto the game board.

2. ____   Nanny stooped, she picked up her poodle.

3. ____   I want juice my friend wants milk.

4. ____   Joe nodded but didn't smile and he waved but didn't come over.

5. ____   Mom went to the gym to work out.

B.   Directions: Rewrite and change these run-on sentences.

1. Penny is an artist she draws cards. _____

2. Wrap this present, put a bow on it. _____

3. She took a bath then went to bed. _____

4. Bo swung and he yelled and he missed the ball but he grinned.

_____

CAPITALIZATION

NOTES

Rule 1: **Capitalize the first word of any sentence.**

A **declarative sentence** makes a statement.

The balloon is silver.

An **imperative sentence** gives a command.

Blow up this balloon.

An **interrogative sentence** asks a question.

Does this balloon have a hole in it?

An **exclamatory sentence** shows emotion or excitement.

You brought us balloons!

Rule 2: **Capitalize a person's name and initials for names.**

Jenny **V**ictoria **S**mith   Jenny **V**. **S**mith   **J. V. S.**

Rule 3: **Capitalize a formal or an informal title.**

Formal Title:
<u>M</u>rs. Jenny **S**mith   <u>D</u>octor Jenny **S**mith   <u>M</u>ayor Jenny **S**mith
<u>C</u>aptain Jenny **S**mith   <u>S</u>enator Jenny **S**mith   <u>J</u>udge Jenny **S**mith

Informal Title:
<u>A</u>unt Jenny   <u>G</u>randma Jenny

Capitalize a title standing alone <u>if</u> a person's name can be inserted.

Did **Dad** give you that?
Insert Dad's name: Did **Tony** give you that?

My **dad** takes us hiking.
You would not say *My Tony takes us hiking*. Do not
capitalize the informal title standing alone here.

Do not capitalize a title if it is a career choice.

Jenny wants to become a doctor.

Rule 4: **Capitalize the pronoun, I.**
(A pronoun takes the place of a noun.)

May **I** show you?

Name_____   **CAPITALIZATION**

Date_____

A. Directions: Write your answers on the line:

1. Write you first, middle, and last names.

   _____ _____ _____

2. Write your initials. _____

3. Write a relative's first name. _____

4. Write your relative's first name with his or her informal title.

         Example: Grammy Tammy   _____

5. Write how your name would appear if you were to become governor of your

    state. _____

6. Write a sentence stating a career choice that you may choose. Use the

    pronoun, *I.* _____

ംഔംഔംഔംഔംഔ

B. Directions: Write the capital letter above any word that needs to be capitalized.

1. may carlos and i speak with the manager?

2. last week miss laura s. finn was hired as a teacher.

3. was president richard m. nixon's middle name millhouse?

4. give uncle troy a hug, parker victoria.

5. i think that dr. minski and mom won the raffle.

6. my grandmother's title and name is representative maria a. trueblood.

7. will dad be interviewing d. t. hooker who is a fire chief?

8. brian and cousin allen bought a tire from mr. pamsky, our neighbor.

9. her uncle and i work in senator shyer's office.

240

Rule 5: **Capitalize days of the week and the months.**

> Examples: **T**hursday   **J**une

Rule 6: **Capitalize holidays and special days.**

> Examples: **P**residents' **D**ay   **A**rbor **D**ay

Rule 7: **Capitalize the proper names of a geographic place.**

> Remember: A common noun names a general topic and is not capitalized.
> A proper noun names a specific person or place.

Examples:

bay - **B**uzzards **B**ay	spring - **H**ot **S**prings
beach - **D**elray **B**each	sound - **V**ineyard **S**ound
canyon - **B**ighorn **C**anyon	state - **I**daho
cape - **C**ape **C**harles	swamp - **C**ongaree **S**wamp
cave - **J**ewel **C**ave	town - **P**edlar **M**ills
city - **H**onolulu	township - **H**ope **T**ownship
creek - **W**hite **R**un	valley - **G**reen **V**alley
continent - **S**outh **A**merica	waterfalls - **A**ngel **F**alls
county - **E**ssex **C**ounty	
dam - **C**oulee **D**am	
desert - **G**reat **S**alt **L**ake **D**esert	
forest - **W**ayne **N**ational **F**orest	
fort - **F**ort **R**aleigh	
gorge - **N**ew **R**iver **G**orge	
gulf - **P**ersian **G**ulf	
harbor - **B**ar **H**arbor	
island - **F**ire **I**sland	
lake - **L**ake **C**helean	
mountain - **M**ount **R**ainier	
ocean - **P**acific **O**cean	
park - **O**lympic **N**ational **P**ark	
pass - **D**eer **L**odge **P**ass	
province - **B**ritish **C**olumbia	
range - **G**rand **T**etons	
recreation area - **L**ake **M**ead **R**ecreation **A**rea	
region - **W**est	
river - **K**nife **R**iver	
ruins - **C**ase **G**rande **R**uins	
sea - **C**aribbean **S**ea	
seashore - **P**adre **I**sland **N**ational **S**eashore	

NOTES

Name_____   **CAPITALIZATION**

Date_____

A. Directions: Write your answers on the line.

1. Write the name of a city that you would like to visit. _____

2. In what state would you like to live someday? _____

3. Name a famous lake. _____

4. Name a country that borders the United States. _____

5. On what continent do you live? _____

6. Name a mountain range. _____

7. What is your favorite park? _____

8. Name a place in Canada. _____

ॐ ॐ ॐ ॐ ॐ

B. Directions: Write the capital letter above any word that needs to be capitalized.

1. is dolphin island in great salt lake?

2. they live near the yew mountains in the east.

3. we visited crystal onyx cave near beaver river in kentucky.

4. last year, we studied about the cumberland falls in daniel boone national forest.

5. is indian springs near amargosa desert in nevada?

6. the fox river empties into green bay.

7. did you know that humbug mountain is located near the pacific ocean?

8. they live in straban township in adams county, pennsylvania.

9. does she visit kure beach near cape fear each summer?

NOTES

Rule 8: **Capitalize the name of canals, tunnels, roads, bridges, monuments, and other structures.**

Examples: **F**ort **M**yers
                Fisher **F**reeway
                Blatnik **B**ridge
                Washington **M**onument
                Harry **G**rove **S**tadium
                Woodlake **N**ature **C**enter

Do not capitalize a TYPE of building. However, if the name of that building is given, capitalize it.

Examples: building - bank   -   **B**ordon **B**ank
                building - museum -   **H**erritt's **M**useum
                building - library -   **M**ercury **L**ibrary
                building - hospital -   **M**emorial **H**ospital

Rule 9: **Capitalize the name of a school, college, or other place of learning.**

Examples: **L**iberty **P**reschool   **M**ercer **U**niversity
                Taft **E**lementary **S**chool   **K**irk **D**ay **S**chool
                West **M**iddle **S**chool   **T**ri **V**ocational **S**chool

Do not capitalize a school, college, or other place of learning if it does not give a specific name.

Examples: Their sister left for college.
                Is Jack attending an art school?

Rule 10: **Capitalize the name of a business.**

Examples: **H**alo **H**air **S**alon   **T**urbo **B**owling **A**lley
                Gentle **G**iant **M**aid **S**ervice   **L**akeside **I**nn
                Gift **B**askets to **Y**ou, Inc.   **A**pple **C**ar **C**ompany
                Deluxe **T**ire **S**tore   **R**aintree **M**all
                Elco **E**nterprises   **A**rc **A**irlines
                Happy **T**rails **R**estaurant   **H**al's **R**anch **S**upplies
                Whitman **T**owing   **P**ride-**L**ee **C**orporation
                Sharon's **C**arpet **C**leaning   **K**ey **C**omputer **S**ervices

Name_____ **CAPITALIZATION**

Date_____

A. Directions: Write your answers on the line.

1. Write the name of the nearest hospital. _____

2. Write the name of your school. _____

3. Create a name for a library. _____

4. What business is closest to your home? _____

5. If you owned your own store, what would you name it?

_____

 app app app app app

B. Directions: Write the capital letter above any word that needs to be capitalized.

1. is egleston children's hospital near atlanta christian college?

2. we crossed memorial bridge instead of taking bismarck expressway.

3. is armstrong tunnel near pittsburgh civic arena?

4. they ate at brookside restaurant before going to belcourt castle in newport.

5. sammy attends muffits preschool on strawberry lane.

6. is quaker hills high school near rock ford plantation?

7. how far is silver stadium from strong museum?

8. their son is a teacher at taft elementary school on rye drive.

9. she flew into bishop airport and drove to baker college.

10. the family stayed at herald hotel near mayfair mall.

11. take interstate 65 to jackson oak monument in mobile, alabama.

12. micah's mom works at birk electric company near his middle school.

Directions: Write the capital letter above any word that needs to be capitalized.

1. marco and i went to silver strand state beach last labor day.

2. we crossed the h. p. long bridge and drove along old spanish trail.

3. have you seen lumbermen's monument in silver valley on lake huron?

4. the happy hen restaurant is located in riverside mall.

5. jana and aunt lulu traveled by cicero swamp to reach everson museum of
    art.

6. next year, governor kaas will visit the great tower in italy.

7. did michelangelo paint the ceiling of the sistine chapel in vatican city?

8. last august, my father began to work for sunshine tile company in clay
    county.

9. the town of iconium is near honey creek state park and rathbun dam.

10. jack attended his cousin's wedding at st. mark's church on saturday,
    march 21.

11. on nurses' day, we visited diamond caverns and picnicked along beaver
    river.

12. did grandpa ganzi attend new jersey training school near interstate 80?

13. candace and her uncle camped near fish creek in mount hood national
    forest.

NOTES

Rule 11: **Capitalize the name of a language.**

    English   **D**utch

    Latin   **G**reek

Rule 12: **Capitalize the name of an organization.**

    Vermont **A**ssociation of **H**ome **E**ducators

    Children's **C**harities **F**oundation

    American **C**ancer **S**ociety

    Paradise **H**ills **R**iding **A**ssociation

Rule 13: **Capitalize the first word of a salutation (greeting) and of a closing of a letter.**

<u>Salutation</u>	<u>Closing</u>
Dear Darby,	**S**incerely yours,
My dearest auntie,	**Y**our best friend,

Rule 14: **Capitalize the name of a special event.**

Prescott **P**ioneer **D**ays	**M**anayunk **A**rts **F**estival
Harney **H**orse **S**how	**G**lendale **D**oll and **B**ear **S**how
American **R**oyal **R**odeo	**B**rown **C**ounty **F**air

    Do NOT capitalize the event <u>unless</u> a specific name is given.

    We attended a bluegrass festival.
    Katrina enjoyed that baby-massage workshop.

Rule 15: **Capitalize the first word in a line of poetry.**

    Fame is fickle food
    Upon a shifting plate . . . .
                  -Emily Dickinson

A. Directions: Write the capital letter above any word that needs to be capitalized.

1. dear reba,

   nicki and i went to clear channel job fair on saturday.

                          love forever,

                          luana

2. do you want to join goldwing riders' club?

3. mom is going to danish days celebration in santa barbara.

4. the country peddler craft show was held in pennsylvania.

5. jasmine speaks only spanish during the oakwood language club meetings.

6. we attended napa valley fair and silverado parade last week.

7. the russian children's welfare society will meet next wednesday.

8. lord alfred tennyson wrote in a poem:

    on either side the river lie,

    long fields of barley and of rye,

9. my friend donated a car to the national kidney foundation last year.

10. some people attending the red poppy festival spoke chinese.

                    ❧❧❧❧❧

B. Directions: Write your answer on the line.

1. What language would you like to learn? _____

2. Write a closing of a letter. _____

250

Rule 16: **Capitalize the name of any historical document.**

    Gettysburg Address

    Voting Rights Act

Rule 17: **Capitalize the name of any historical event.**

    Battle of Quebec

    Whiskey Rebellion

Rule 18: **Capitalize the name of a government body or organization.**

    Supreme Court   House of Representatives

    Congress   Department of Treasury

Rule 19: **Capitalize the name of a program.**

    Great Frontier

    Head Start

    Operation Smile

Rule 20: **Capitalize the name of a colony, empire, or other governments.**

    Plymouth Colony   Xia Dynasty

    Bear Flag Republic   United States of America

Rule 21: **Capitalize the name of a political party and members of a political party.**

    Progressive Party   a Democrat

    a Republican candidate

Rule 22: **Capitalize the name of a period of time.**

    Air Age

    Era of Good Feelings

NOTES

Name_____   **CAPITALIZATION**

Date_____

Directions: Write the capital letter above any word that needs to be capitalized.

1. did congress pass the hepburn act to regulate railroads?

2. after the lone star republic became texas, the mexican war was fought.

3. where people could not read in america, the *constitution* was read to them.

4. the virginia colony was first a part of the british empire.

5. during the revolutionary war, the battle of savannah was fought in georgia.

6. the department of housing and urban development was created to aid cities.

7. in 1956, the interstate highway program was started to build 41,000 miles of

    divided highways.

8. during the middle ages, marco polo visited the chinese empire.

9. the north atlantic treaty organization was formed in 1949.

10. the members of the populist party joined democrats in nominating william j.

    bryan.

11. the qing dynasty was followed by the republic of china in 1912.

12. after world war II, the government of puerto rico started a project called

    "operation bootstrap" to help the people.

13. after the french and indian war, britain and france signed the treaty of

    paris.

14. did the jefferson parent organization sponsor the helping children program?

Directions: Write the capital letter above any word that needs to be capitalized.

1. the roman empire began when the roman senate named a leader.

2. was the geneva agreement of 1954 also written in Japanese?

3. poetry: pink clouds

    light blue sky

    sunset on the horizon

4. we attend the merritt mountain music festival each year.

5. president johnson belonged to the whig party after the civil war.

6. his family went to the san jose air show.

7. she belongs to the buckles and bows square dance club.

8. the peace corps was started under kennedy's program called the new

    frontier.

9. is the head of children's toy foundation speaking at a meeting tonight?

10. during the space age, a woman from the soviet union went into orbit.

11. does the leader of the international trade organization speak german?

12. the national defense education act helped young people go to college.

13. dear wyatt,

      did you go to the dover film festival recently? i heard they

      showed a film about the war of 1812.

                                        your buddy,
254   than

Rule 23: **Capitalize the first word of a direct quotation** (that which a person says). **The person who said it must also be included.**

> Example: Selena said, "**M**y science project fizzled."

Note that the word after the direct quotation is **not** capitalized unless it is a person's name or another proper noun.

> Example: "**W**here is your dog?" **a**sked Julio.

Rule 24: **Capitalize the first word, the last word, and all important words of a title.**

> Examples: <u>**N**ight **F**lying</u>
> "**M**y **B**ig **T**eddy **B**ear"

How do you know if a word is **important** and should be capitalized?

This will help you: <u>**Do not capitalize *a, an, the, and, but, or, nor,* or *prepositions of four or less letters* (unless the word is first or last).**</u>

> Examples: <u>**B**abe, the **G**allant **P**ig</u>
> "**T**he **K**ing and **H**is **H**arp"

Rule 25: **Capitalize the Roman numerals and the letters of the major topics in an outline.**

> I.
>   A.
>   B.
>   C.
>
> II.
>   A.
>   B.
>   C.

Capitalize the first word in an outline. If other words in the outline are proper nouns, capitalize them. Otherwise, no other words are capitalized.

> I.   **A**dvertising in print
>   A.   **D**irect mail
>   B.   **I**n stores
> II.   **C**ommercials in **E**nglish

NOTES

Name_____

Date_____

A. Directions: Capitalize these titles.

1. hatchet

2. national velvet

3. "america the beautiful"

4. no dogs allowed

5. the boxcar children

6. "the farmer in the dell"

7. anne of green gables

8. "the land and the people"

ক্তক্তক্তক্তক্তক্ত

B. Directions: Capitalize this outline.

     i. evening clothing

        a. formal wear

           1. tuxedos

           2. cocktail dresses

        b. casual clothes

    ii. special attire

        a. bridal gowns

        b. prom gowns

ক্তক্তক্তক্তক্তক্ত

C. Directions: Write the capital letter where needed.

1. marsha asked, "what would you like to drink?"

2. "you must sit down," said paco.

3. captain john smith said, "if you don't work, you don't eat."

4. "this is my best project!" exclaimed hunter.

5. william shakespeare wrote the line, "to be or not to be · · · ·."

NOTES

Rule 26: Capitalize a brand name but not the product.

      Examples: **P**opo paper towels

                     Stonybrook bread

Rule 27: Capitalize the name of a religion and the name for a supreme being.

      Examples: **J**udaism   **G**od

                     Christianity   **H**eavenly **F**ather

                     Hindu   **B**uddha

Rule 28: Capitalize the name of a church, temple, or other place of worship.

      Examples: **I**glesia de **D**ios

                     Tempe **C**alvary **C**hurch

                     Mt. **S**inai **T**emple

Rule 29: Capitalize the name of a religious denomination.

      Examples: **P**resbyterian   **L**utheran

If the name of a specific church is **not** given, capitalize only the denomination.

      Example: a **M**ormon mission

Rule 30: Capitalize a proper adjective but not the noun it modifies.

      Remember: A proper adjective comes from a proper noun.

PROPER NOUN	PROPER ADJECTIVE
France	French
Asia	**A**sian

      Examples: a **F**rench inn

                     an **A**sian country

Rule 31: Capitalize a direction when it refers to a region of a country or a region of the world. Capitalize a direction when it is used with a specific geographic place.

      Examples: He lives in the **N**orthwest.

                     Their daughter is in the **M**iddle **E**ast.

                     My address is 12 **N**orth Elm Lane.

A. Directions: Write your answers on the line.

1. Make up a name for a brand of milk. _____

2. Name a church, synagogue, or other place of worship in your area.

_____

3. What is the proper adjective for *Alaska*? _____

4. In which region of the country do you live? _____

5. Name a religion of the world. _____

6. Do you live in the Eastern Hemisphere or Western Hemisphere?

_____

చు చు చు చు చు చు చు చు చు చు చు

B. Directions: Place capital letters where needed.

1. my aunt bought a wislow* tractor for her virginia home.

2. is st. peter's episcopal church located at 509 east orange avenue?

3. kami purchased an african table and a risca* baking dish at a yard sale.

4. her european friend visited the south recently.

5. a quilt sale was held at a baptist church on west adams street.

6. his uncle visited a shinto temple on an american island.

7. sal grew up in a german neighborhood in the east.

8. does buddhism include a belief about goddesses?

9. is zeus a god in greek or roman mythology?

*a brand name

DO NOT CAPITALIZE

animals: **frog**   **fox**

However, capitalize a proper adjective with an animal.

Example: Shawn has an **I**rish setter.   (country - **I**reland)

dances: **tap dance**   **waltz**

However, capitalize a proper adjective with a dance.

Example: We like the **M**exican hat dance. (country - **M**exico)

directions: **north**   **southeast**

However, capitalize a direction if it is a region of the country or a region of the world.

Examples: They visit the **N**ortheast.

Lebanon is in the **N**ear **E**ast.

In addition, capitalize a direction when it appears with a geographic place.

Examples: His father went to **N**orth **K**orea.

They live at 20 **E**ast **C**obbler **S**treet

diseases: **cold**   **cancer**

However, capitalize a proper adjective with a disease.

Examples: My grandma once had the **A**sian flu.

(continent - **A**sia)

The patient has **A**lzheimer's disease.

(**A**lzheimer was the one who "discovered" the disease.)

261

foods: **ham**   **peach**

> **However**, capitalize a proper adjective with a food.
>
> > Example: May I have a **D**anish pastry?
> >
> > > (country - **D**enmark)

career choices: **nurse**   **police officer**

games: **checkers**   **puzzles**

> **However**, capitalize a trademarked game.
>
> > Example: We played **R**ummicub.

musical instruments: **drum**   **clarinet**

> **However**, capitalize a proper adjective with a musical instrument.
>
> > Example: Mrs. Boca plays the **F**rench horn. (country - France)

seasons: **autumn**   **summer**

school subjects: **reading**   **history**

> **However**, capitalize a proper adjective with a school subject.
>
> > Example: **A**merican history
>
> **In addition**, capitalize a subject if it is a language or has a number.
>
> > Examples: **E**nglish
> >
> >   **A**lgebra II

plants: **pansy**   **bush**

> **However**, capitalize a proper adjective with a plant.
>
> > Example: **E**nglish tea rose

262

Name_____   **CAPITALIZATION**

Date_____

Directions: You have learned that there are certain categories that we do not
                     capitalize. Unscramble the words that name these.

Do not capitalize:

1.   aesssno - _ _ _ _ _ _ _

2.   esssidae - _ _ _ _ _ _ _ _

3.   uscamli nutrsnsitem - _ _ _ _ _ _ _   _ _ _ _ _ _ _ _ _ _

4.   ncodetriis - _ _ _ _ _ _ _ _ _ _

5.   eerrac oiehccs - _ _ _ _ _ _ _   _ _ _ _ _ _ _

6.   adnsec - _ _ _ _ _ _

7.   snamisal - _ _ _ _ _ _ _

8.   emgsa - _ _ _ _ _

9.   closho butscejs - _ _ _ _ _ _   _ _ _ _ _ _ _ _

10.   odosf - _ _ _ _ _

11.   saplnt - _ _ _ _ _ _

Directions: Write the capital letter above any word that needs to be capitalized.

1. my favorite subjects are english and arithmetic.

2. One of her uncles who has tonsillitis lives in the south.

3. his german shepherd was playing under a weeping willow tree.

4. she dances the polka while her uncle plays the accordion.

5. have you every played chess during your summer vacation?

6. chan lives at 647 south ritz avenue in the northeast.

7. their dad became district manager of a southwest company.

8. our little beagle should never be fed chocolate candy.

9. grandpa planted cherry tomatoes and bermuda onions in his garden.

10. the couple danced the tango as the man played a portuguese mandolin.

11. the principal of that school also teaches earth science and biology I.

12. a scottish chef made crepes and used a german caramel sauce.

13. last autumn, allie visited her grandparents in west virginia.

14. in music class, we learned about the french horn, the trombone, and the

     oboe.

Directions: Write the capital letter above any word that needs to be capitalized.

1. a. "baby tortoise"   c. mistakes that worked

    b. the dark stories   d. danger at the fair

2. many people who live in montreal, canada, speak french.

3. the romanov dynasty in russia ruled for over three hundred years.

4. the federalist papers were written by james madison and john jay.

5. dear uncle mario,

        the sports car club of germany will meet in november at braun

    house.

                                            sincerely yours,

                                            anthony

6. "give your speech on armed forces day,"   said his granddad.

7. did the pullman company fire workers join the american railway

    union?

8. is the monsoon golf tournament held at graystone country club?

9. they went to st. vincent island near cape saint george.

10. in december, dad traveled to highland lake along the maine turnpike.

11. the arctic circle is south of the brooks range and near the bering sea.

12. dr. allison r. jones asked, "have you had hay fever or a sinus infection?"

NOTES

PUNCTUATION

NOTES

PERIOD: (.)

Rule 1: Place a period at the end of a declarative sentence.

A **declarative sentence** makes a statement.

This wrench is rusted.

Rule 2: Place a period at the end of an imperative sentence.

An **imperative sentence** gives a command.

Stand up.

Rule 3: Place a period after most abbreviations.

A. Days of the Week:

Sunday -- **Sun.**
Monday — **Mon.**
Tuesday — **Tues., Tue.***
Wednesday — **Wed.**

Thursday — **Thurs., Thur.***
Friday — **Fri.**
Saturday — **Sat.**

*The first listing is preferred.

B. Months of the Year:

January — **Jan.**
February — **Feb.**
March — **Mar.**
April — **Apr.**
May
June

July
August — **Aug.**
September — **Sept.**
October — **Oct.**
November — **Nov.**
December — **Dec.**

C. Titles and Initials:

Ms. — title that does not show if a woman is married or unmarried

Mrs. — (plural = Mmes.) title before a married woman's name

Mr. — Mister

Juan Victor Sanchez — **J. V. S.**   **Mr. J. V. S**anchez

Pres. (**P**resident) Sanchez   **Gov.** (**G**overnor) Sanchez

D. Places (general):

Drive — **Dr.**   Street — **St.**   Highway — **Hwy.**
Avenue — **Ave.**   Lane — **Ln.**   Boulevard — **Blvd.**

CHECK A DICTIONARY IF YOU ARE UNSURE OF AN ABBREVIATION.

NOTES

PERIOD: (.) cont.

    E. Places (specific):

Saint Paul — **St. Paul**	Mount Fox — **Mt. Fox**
Minnesota — **Minn.**	North America — **N. Am.**

However, do not place a period after a postal code: Minnesota - **MN**

    F. Directions:

       North — **N.**   southwest — **sw.**

    G. Organizations:

Some organizations use periods with their abbreviations.
American Dairy Science Association — **A. D. S. A.**

The abbreviation of many organizations no longer require periods.
County Dance and Song Society — **CDSS**
Association of Christian Schools International — **ACSI**

When the abbreviation spells a word (acronym), periods are not used.
Educational Concerns for Hunger Organization — **ECHO**

    H. Others:

abbreviation — **abbrev.**	approximately — **approx.**
Swedish — **Swed.**	Before Christ — **B.C.**
adverb — **adv.**	Anno Domino (Latin = in the year of the Lord) — **A.D.**

NOTE: **If a sentence ends with an abbreviation that requires a period, do not place another period.**   He addressed me as Mrs.

Rule 4: Place a period after the letters and numbers in outlines.

     I. Marine animals
        A. Squid
        B. Starfish
    II. Land animals
        A. Camels
            1. One-Humped
            2. Two-Humped
        B. Elephants

Name_____   **PUNCTUATION**

Date_____   **Periods**

Directions: Write your answer on each line.

1.   Write your first, middle, and last names.   _____

2.   Write your initials.   _____

3.   Write your state's postal code.   _____

4.   Using abbreviations, write 13 West Ark Street.   _____

5.   Write the abbreviation for each day of the week: _____   _____

     _____   _____   _____   _____   _____

6.   Write the abbreviation for each month: January - _____   February - _____

     March - _____   April - _____   August - _____   September - ____

     October - _____   November - _____   December - _____

7.   Using the abbreviation for doctor, write a friend's name if he or she were to

     become a physician.   _____

8.   Write an abbreviation for the National Hockey League.   _____

9.   Using an abbreviation, name a mountain.   _____

10.   Place periods in this outline: I   North America
                                            A   Canada
                                                1   Government
                                                2   Tourism
                                            B   Mexico
                                        II   South America
                                            A   Peru
                                            B   Argentina
                                            C   Chile
                                                1   Geography
                                                2   Resources

272

Directions: Place a period where needed.

1. Turn on the light

2. Mrs Tang and Gov Reed will meet soon

3. His home is at 125 S Denver St

4. They traveled to Ft McDowell last week

5. I lived in St Louis, MO, when I was a child

6. Lieut Deanna P Vanderhall is stationed in Eur for two years

7.   On Sat , Jan 1, they'll release a new album

8. I   Pioneer men

    A   Daniel Boone

       1   Life

       2   Travels

    B   Davy Crockett

  II   Pioneer women

    A   Jenny Wiley

    B   Abigail Dunway

    C   Elizabeth Hamrick

9. The Battle of Hastings occurred in 1066 A D

10. Ms Lyon, do you live on E Princess Dr ?

COMMA: (,)

Rule 1:   Place a comma between the day and year in a date.

November 30, 2010

Rule 2:   Place a comma between a day and date.

Tuesday, April23, 2002

Rule 3:   Place a comma after a date if the date doesn't end a sentence.

They married on May 15, 2004, in Boston.

෴෴෴෴෴෴෴෴෴෴෴෴

A.   Directions: Write the answer.

1.   Write the month, day, and year that you were born (in words and numbers).

_____

2.   Write the name of the day, month, day (number) and year of tomorrow's date.

_____

3.   Look at *Rule 3*. Write a date within a sentence.

_____

෴෴෴෴෴෴෴෴෴෴෴෴

B.   Directions: Insert commas where needed.

1.   Are you attending their wedding on December 2 2008?

2.   Katie graduated on Friday June 7 2002.

3.   On March 4 2011 our neighbors will celebrate their twenty-fifth wedding anniversary.

274

COMMA: (,)

Rule 4: **Place a comma between a town or city and a state.**

Orlando, Florida

Rule 5: **Place a comma between a town and a county.**

Gettysburg, Adams County

Rule 6: **Place a comma between a city and a country.**

Madrid, Spain

Rule 7: **In a street address, place a comma after the street and after the city. Do not place a comma between a state and zip code.**

Their address is 34 Rice Lane, Lenexa, KS   66215.

Do **not** place a comma *if* a word appears between the street address and city.

Their address is 34 Rice Lane **in** Lenexa, KS   66215.

Note that a comma is **not** placed between the *house address* and the street address.

Their address is *34* Rice Lane, Lenexa, KS   66215.

Rule 8: **Place a comma after the state or country if it appears before the end of a sentence.**
Min lived in Fairfax, Virginia, for ten years.

ॐॐॐॐॐॐॐॐॐॐ

Directions: Write the answer.

1. Write a sentence stating your complete address. (Include your zip code.)

   _____

2. Using *Rule 5,* write a sentence with your town (city) and state appearing within the sentence.

   _____

Directions: Insert commas where needed.

1. Jemima moved to Fairbanks Alaska.

2. Mrs. Remus was hired on July 5 2004.

3. Was President George W. Bush sworn into office on Monday January 2 2000?

4. Jacob's friend moved to 5 Mill Road in Mount Laurel New Jersey.

5. Their uncle lives at 12 Wilmot Road Tucson Arizona   85711.

6. The mayor resigned on Tuesday October 5 2004.

7. The museum will open in Orange County California.

8. The conference was held on November 2 2004 in Casper Wyoming.

9. Miss Firth's office is at 4 Marsh Road Wilmington DE 19810.

10. The board meeting was held on Friday August 22 2004 at noon.

11. Marco and Anne live in Miami Dade County Florida.

12. We traveled to Toledo Ohio last winter.

COMMA: (,)

Rule 9: **Place a comma after three or more items in a series. Do not place a comma <u>after the last item</u>.**

I'll buy boots, a ski jacket, and gloves for our trip.

Rule 10: **Place a comma after an introductory word.**

No, I'm not ready.   Yes, I can hear you.   Well, I think so.

Rule 11: **Place a comma after the greeting of a friendly letter.**

Dear Tate,

Rule 12: **Place a comma after the closing of a friendly letter.**

Yours truly,

Rule 13: **Place a comma to set off a noun of direct address** (a person spoken "to").

Carla, may I go with you?   May I go with you, Carla?

If a noun of direct address is within a sentence, place a comma **before** and **after** it.

May I, Carla, go with you?

෴෴෴෴෴෴෴෴෴෴෴෴

Directions: Insert needed commas.

1. No we aren't leaving at noon.

2. Hannah will you show me your picture?

3. Dear Rob
       I am glad that you are bringing juice rolls and hot dogs to our picnic. Yes you may bring your friend along. I'll see you there Cousin Rob.
                                          Always
                                          Chan   277

COMMA: (,)

Rule 9: **Place a comma after three or more items in a series. Do not place a comma <u>after the last item</u>.**

Fruit pops, water, and yogurt were sold at the fair.

Rule 10: **Place a comma after an introductory word.**

Yes, we are sure.

Rule 11: **Place a comma after the greeting of a friendly letter.**

My friend,

Rule 12: **Place a comma after the closing of a friendly letter.**

Truly yours,

Rule 13: **Place a comma to set off a noun of direct address** (a person spoken "to").

Jenny, sit with us.   Sit with us, Jenny.

If a noun of direct address is within a sentence, place a comma **before** and **after** it.

Sit, Jenny, with us.

☙☙☙☙☙☙☙☙☙☙☙

Directions: Insert needed commas.

1. Dear Nan

Yes I can come with you to Yellowstone.

Your best friend
Devi

2. Micah will you compete in Brazilian jujitsu?

3. The dancer placed her tap shoes her ballet shoes and a comb in her bag.

278

COMMA: (,)

Rule 14:   Use a comma to clarify (make clear) a sentence.

Within the candle bits of colored wax floated.
Within the candle, bits of colored wax floated.

Rule 15:   Use a comma to invert a name. Place the last name, a comma, and the first name.

Kesi A. Contos   =   Contos, Kesi A.

Rule 16:   If two complete sentences are joined by a conjunction *(and, but, or)*, place a comma before the conjunction.

You may take an oatmeal cookie, or you may choose a yogurt.

Rule 17:   Use a comma after a direct quotation that is followed by a verb like "said" and a speaker. (It will not ask a question or show emotion.)

"This offer is reasonable," said the seller.

If the person who is making the statement is given first, place a comma after the person's name + verb. (This may use "asked" or "exclaimed.")

Kissa remarked, "That is not true."

Elias asked, "Where is my wallet?"

Rule 18:   Use a comma to set off an appositive. (An appositive is a word or group of words that explains a noun in a sentence. Often, an appositive will give additional information about the noun.)

Tama likes her job.   (Who is *Tama*?)

Tama, <u>my aunt</u>, likes her job.

ৰ৵ৰ৵ৰ৵ৰ৵ৰ৵ৰ৵ৰ৵ৰ৵ৰ৵ৰ৵ৰ৵

Directions: Insert needed commas.

1.   The mechanic asked "Where's my wrench?"

2.   Mrs. Hart our neighbor has been elected mayor.

3.   Before dinner plates must be set on this table.

4.   "Please come in " said Emily.

COMMA: (,)

> **Rule 14:   Use a comma to clarify (make clear) a sentence.**
>
>> After the party favors were given.
>> After the party, favors were given.
>
> **Rule 15:   Use a comma to invert a name. Place the last name, a comma, and the first name.**
>> Tom J. Lee   =   Lee, Tom J.
>
> **Rule 16:   If two complete sentences are joined by a conjunction (*and, but, or*), place a comma before the conjunction.**
>
>> His motorcycle is old, but it looks new and shiny.
>
> **Rule 17:   Use a comma after a direct quotation that is followed by a verb like "said" and a speaker.** (It will not ask a question or show emotion.)
>
>> "This avocado is too ripe," said Lars.
>
> **If the person who is making the statement is given first, place a comma after the person's name + verb.** (This may use "asked" or "exclaimed.")
>
>> Lars said, "This avocado is too ripe."
>
>> Emma asked, "Is this avocado too ripe?"
>
> **Rule 18:   Use a comma to set off an appositive.** (An appositive is a word or group of words that explains a noun in a sentence. Often, an appositive will give additional information about the noun.)
>
>> Bo likes to sit on the front step.   (Who is *Bo*?)
>
>> Bo, <u>our kitty</u>, likes to sit on the front step.

వ్ఴ వ్ఴ వ్ఴ వ్ఴ వ్ఴ వ్ఴ వ్ఴ వ్ఴ వ్ఴ వ్ఴ వ్ఴ

Directions: Insert needed commas.

1.   Brad's name on the list appeared as Smith Brad.

2.   "I want up " said the toddler.

3.   Give this hat to Miss Lant the lady in the red hat.

4.   The bride walked down the aisle and she waved to her nephews.

Directions: Insert needed commas.

1. Lindy

    Shari's wedding is on Sunday December 21 2006.

                              Love
                              Annie

2. You look like your mother and your brother looks like your dad.

3. Johnson Ricky T.

4. The car attendant asked "May I have your keys?"

5. My new home is at 12 Ruby Lane Rockford IL 61102.

6. No I won't be flying to Rome Italy.

7. Mrs. Reed do you want to buy a cookbook?

8. Her family's pets include a ferret a hamster a cat and three dogs.

9. Ted arrived from Memphis Tennessee this morning.

10. In the middle of the storm clouds billowed overhead.

11. "You stepped in some mud " said his mother.

12.   Mom said "We must go to the grocery store Kim."

13. Chessa my little sister in the white dress is a flower girl.

14. Jessica has bought a new bike but she will ride it only on trails.

15. "The wood on this gate needs to be replaced " said the carpenter.

16.   Mark will attend Baylor University or he will go to a college in his state.

17. Her dog a small Scotch terrier is groomed at La Pierre's.

Question Mark:

Rule: Use a question mark (?) at the end of an interrogative sentence. (An interrogative sentence asks a question.)

Did Madison find her hockey stick**?**
Will you come with me**?**

Exclamation Mark:

Rule 1: Use an exclamation point (!) after an exclamatory sentence. (An *exclamatory sentence* shows strong feeling.)

We're the first-place winners!
Mom, I just saw a snake!

Rule 2: Use an exclamation point (!) after an interjection.
(An *interjection* is a word <u>or</u> phrase that shows strong feeling.)

Cool! Let's do it!
I lost my wallet! *Oh no!*

phrase – two or more words that do not
form a complete sentence

꙰꙰꙰꙰꙰꙰꙰꙰꙰꙰꙰꙰꙰꙰꙰꙰꙰꙰

Part A: Place question marks or exclamation marks where needed.

1. Yikes I almost stepped on a toad

2. Have you eaten lunch

3. You're the champion

Part B: Write a sentence using the required ending punctuation.

1. (question mark)

   _____

   _____

2. (exclamation point)

   _____

   _____

Apostrophe:

Rule 1: Use an apostrophe (') in a contraction to show where a letter or letters have been left out.

> can't - cannot
> I'm - I am

Rule 2: Use an apostrophe (') to show possession (ownership).

> **A. If the word showing ownership is singular (one), add ' + s.**
>
> > a kitten**'s** pillow
> > the book**'s** cover
> > one model**'s** smile
>
> **B. If the word showing ownership is plural (more than one) and ends in s, just add an apostrophe after the s.**
>
> > one lady - many ladies: ladies' tea rooms
> > one bee - two bees: bees' hive
>
> **C. If the word showing ownership is plural (more than one) and does NOT end in s, add ' + s.**
>
> > one mouse - two mice: mice**'s** nest
> > one child - many children: children**'s** books

ぬぬぬぬぬぬぬぬぬぬぬぬ

Directions: Write the following.

1. a contraction - _____

2. watercolors belonging to a boy - _____

3. cakes from several bakeries - _____

4. shoes belonging to more than one repairman - _____

5. a wagon belonging to Les - _____

Apostrophe:

Rule 1: Use an apostrophe (') in a contraction to show where a letter or letters have been left out.

> they're - they are
> don't - do not

Rule 2: Use an apostrophe (') to show possession (ownership).

> **A. If the word showing ownership is singular (one), add ' + s.**
>
> > a tassle on a rope - rope**'s** tassle
> > one cowgirl**'s** boots

> **B. If the word showing ownership is plural (more than one) and ends in s, just add an apostrophe (') after the s.**
>
> a trailer - many trailers: trailers' hitches
> one boy - many boys: boys' club

> **C. If the word showing ownership is plural (more than one) and does NOT end in s, add ' + s.**
>
> one goose - two geese: geese**'s** meadow
> businesswoman - two businesswomen: businesswomen**'s** meeting

When two people own the *same* item, add an apostrophe after the second name.

> Example: Katie and Lani's new apartment

When two people own *separate* items, add an apostrophe after both names.

> Example: Tim's and Tate's cars

🐎🐎🐎🐎🐎🐎🐎🐎🐎🐎🐎

Directions: Insert needed apostrophes.

1. My bicycles tire is flat.

2. If youre ready to leave, Ill drive you home.

3. Mary and Jonahs aunt wouldnt go on the ride.

4. Womens dresses and toddlers shoes are on sale today.

5. Didnt her mother buy a mans suit?

COLON: (:)

Rule 1: Use a colon in writing the time.

        4:30 A.M.   9:19 P.M.

Rule 2: Use a colon to break down larger units to smaller ones.

        Genesis 1:1   Unit 5: Chapter 3

Rule 3: Place a colon after divisions of topics in writing.

        Animals:

          Jungle Animals:

Rule 4: Place a colon after the greeting of a business letter.

        Dear Senator Kane: Gentlemen:

Rule 5: Use a colon after the heading of a list.

        Things to do:
- Walk the dog
- Do homework

The clerk ordered the following: lipstick, eye shadow, blush, and liner.

      ཀྵ

Directions: Write an example for each rule.

Rule 1: _____

Rule 2: _____

Rule 3: _____

Rule 4: _____

Rule 5: _____

Colon:

Rule 1: **Use a colon in writing the time.**   7:05 P.M.

Rule 2: **Use a colon to break down larger units to smaller ones.**

Numbers 3:1   Chapter 2: Part 1

Rule 3: **Place a colon after divisions of topics in writing.**

Battles:
  Battle of Bull Run:

Rule 4: **Place a colon after the greeting of a business letter.** Madam:

Rule 5: **Use a colon after the heading of a list.**

Things I want:
- Video
- CD
- Vinyl

Did you buy these items: cereal, milk, bread, butter, and grapes?

Directions: Place a colon where needed.

1. Names of my dogs
    - Rex
    - Sugar
    - Force

2. Dear Mr. Benson

3. You must return these items to the public library a video, a book and a DVD.

4. Things to remember
    - Call my friend
    - Meet my brother after school
    - Help wash the car

5. Please be ready by 4 00 in the afternoon.

> **Reminder:** A **complete sentence** can stand alone as a
> **complete thought.**

Semicolon:

**Rule: Use a semicolon (;) to join two complete sentences. These must
be about a similar topic.**

Correct: Jana is on a swim team; she practices at a nearby pool.

Incorrect: Jana is on a swim team; her uncle lives in Nebraska.

complete sentence   complete sentence

*Note: Place the semicolon after the last word of the first thought.
Place the first word of the second complete thought a space
after the semicolon.*

Example: The boys went fishing; they didn't catch any fish.

🐚🐚🐚🐚🐚🐚🐚🐚🐚🐚🐚🐚🐚🐚🐚🐚🐚🐚

Part A: Place a semicolon after the first complete thought. Write a complete
sentence that is about the same topic on the line.

1. Lee is a carpenter _____.

2. They have a new puppy _____.

3. Lana and I saw little lambs on a farm _____.

4. I can't find my pen _____.

5. Their mom is a good baker _____.

Part B: Place a semicolon between the complete thoughts.

1. A rooster crowed loudly it woke me.

2. Bo and I are going to the beach we are leaving at nine o'clock in the morning.

3. Lynx Lake is in Arizona it is located near the city of Prescott.

4. These glass vases are colorful they are considered works of art.

Semicolon:

Rule: Use a semicolon (;) to join two complete sentences. These must be about a similar topic. Do <u>not</u> place a conjunction (*and, but, or*) with a semicolon.

      Correct: Lars is a toddler; he just learned to walk.

      <u>**Incorrect:**</u>   Lars is a toddler; and he just learned to walk.

      Correct: Katie found a quarter on the floor; she didn't spend it.

      <u>**Incorrect**</u>:   Katie found a quarter on the floor; but she didn't spend it.

                ം⌇ം⌇ം⌇ം⌇ം⌇ം⌇ം⌇ം⌇ം⌇ം⌇ം⌇ം⌇ം⌇ം⌇ം⌇ം⌇ം⌇ം⌇ം⌇

Part A: Place a semicolon after the first complete thought. Write a complete sentence that is about the same topic after the semicolon.

Remember: Place the semicolon after the last word of the first thought.
Place the first word of the second complete thought a space after the semicolon.

1. They placed a fan on their patio _____.

2. The child scraped her knee _____.

3. The day had turned cold _____.

4. We put pink light bulbs in our lamp _____.

5. Grandma lives in a gated house _____.

Part B: Place a semicolon between the complete thoughts.

1. Tom bought a new tub it is round with jet sprays.

2. A stagecoach ran along that route someone built a hotel for travelers.

3. These flowers are drooping they need water.

4. Several farmers are growing figs others are growing olives.

288

REVIEW

Semicolon:
Rule: Use a semicolon (;) to join two complete sentences.
These must be about a similar topic.

Colon:
Rule 1: Use a colon (:) in writing the time.   12:00 A.M.

Rule 2: Use a colon (:) to break down units.   Mark 3:10
Chapter 3: Part 2

Rule 3: Place a colon (:) after divisions of topics in writing.   Lakes:
Salt:

Rule 4: Place a colon after the greeting of a business letter.   Dear Sir:

Rule 5: Use a colon after the heading of a list.   Camping List:
- flashlight
- sleeping bag
- water bottles

This is my camping list **(:)** a flashlight, a sleeping bag, and water bottles.

Directions: Place semicolons and colons where needed.

1. Rule 1 Wait your turn.

2. You will need the following items by noon   a sack lunch, snacks, and drinks.

3. This hat is old it belonged to my poppa.

4. Dad read Psalm 10 3 at the 11 00 church service.

5. Landforms
Islands
Coves

6. Members of the Board

7. Her poodle has a bow on its collar it must have been groomed.

Hyphen:

Rule 1:   Use a hyphen (-) to combine some closely related words.

half-moon   top-notch

Use a dictionary to determine if words should use a hyphen.

Rule 2:   Use a hyphen (-) between fractions.

one-third   three-fourths

Rule 3:   Use a hyphen (-) between two-digit word numbers from 21 to 99.

twenty-one   eighty-five

Rule 4:   Use a hyphen (-) when dividing a word of two or more syllables when they are at the end of a line of writing.

Remember: Words are divided into units of sound called *syllables*.

Important: You must have at least <u>2</u> letters on the first line.

_____**ab-**

sent_____

You must have at least <u>3</u> letters on the second line

_____dangerous-

Wrong: **ly**_____

_____danger-

Right: **ously**_____

Use a dictionary to determine where words will be divided into syllables.

Directions: Write your answer on the line.

1.   Write two words that use a hyphen: _____

2.   Write a fraction in the first space and a two-digit number in the second:

_____   _____

3.   Write a two-syllable word that uses the fourth rule: _____

_____

290

Hyphen:
Rule 1: **Use a hyphen (-) to combine some closely related words.**

three-cornered   triple-play

Use a dictionary to determine if words should use a hyphen.

Rule 2: **Use a hyphen (-) between fractions.**

one-eighth   three-sevenths

Rule 3: **Use a hyphen (-) between two-digit word numbers from 21 to 99.**

forty-two   fifty-five

Rule 4: **Use a hyphen (-) when dividing a word of two or more syllables when they are at the end of a line of writing.**
Remember: Words are divided into units of sound called *syllables*.

Important: **You must have at least 2 letters on the first line.**
_____ **tri-**
cycle _____

You must have at least 3 letters on the second line
_____ **yell-**
ing _____
Use a dictionary to determine where words will be divided into syllables.

ᕙᕗᕙᕗᕙᕗᕙᕗᕙᕗᕙᕗᕙᕗᕙᕗᕙᕗᕙᕗᕙᕗ

Directions: Place a hyphen where needed.

1. My two toned hair looks odd.

2. Their aunt will be thirty seven next month.

3. She received twenty four two toned roses.

4. Mix one half cup of water with cornstarch.

5. Our grandfather's tool set has a large, wooden ham
     mer called a mallet.

Underlining:

Rule 1:   Underline the name of an airplane, a ship, or a train.

ship, <u>Queen Mary</u>

If you are typing an underlined word, you may *italicize* it.   ship, *Queen Mary*

Rule 2:   Underline the letter(s), word(s), or number(s) out of context.

Your <u>2</u> in the address needs to be larger.
Make your <u>S</u> with a smaller loop.

If you are typing an underlined word, you may *italicize* it.

Your *2* in the address needs to be larger.
Make your *S* with a smaller loop.

Rule 3:   Underline the title of a book, magazine, movie, newspaper, play, television show, CD/tape/vinyl album, work of art, sculpture, opera, and long poem.

Easy Grammar **Note: An item is usually underlined if you can receive it separately in the mail.**

book – <u>Slim and Miss Prim</u>   television show - <u>Zoom</u>
magazine – <u>Highlights</u>   movie – <u>Spirit</u>
newspaper – <u>London Times</u>   play – <u>Peter Pan</u>
CD/tape/vinyl album - <u>Arriving</u>   work of art – <u>Yakama Dancer</u>
sculpture – <u>Venus de Milo</u>   opera – <u>Aida</u>

In print, a title will be in *italics* rather than underlined.

Have you read *Slim and Miss Prim*?

🐎🐎🐎🐎🐎🐎🐎🐎🐎🐎🐎🐎🐎🐎🐎🐎🐎🐎

Directions: Write the following titles:

1. Name of a book - _____

2. Name of a movie - _____

3. Name of a television show - _____

4. Name of a play or an album - _____

292

Underlining:

Rule 1: Underline the name of an airplane, a ship, or a train.

train – <u>Thomas</u>

If you are typing an underlined word, you may _italicize_ it.   _Thomas_

Rule 2: Underline the letter(s), word(s), or number(s) out of context.

You forgot a <u>3</u> in your sum.

If you are typing an underlined word, you may _italicize_ it.

You forgot a _3_ in your sum.

Rule 3: Underline the title of a book, magazine, movie, newspaper, play, television show, CD/tape/vinyl album, work of art, sculpture, opera, and long poem.

Easy Grammar Note: An item is usually underlined if you can receive it separately in the mail.

Her favorite book is <u>The Very Hungry Caterpillar</u>.

In print, a title will be in _italics_ rather than underlined.

Her favorite book is _The Very Hungry Caterpillar_.

Directions: Underline where needed.

1.   Is Dad reading The Copywriter's Handbook?

2.   Dot your i in your first word, Tomas.

3.   Their family likes to watch reruns of Happy Days.

4.   Do you know the color of the train, Percy?

5.   Have you listened to the CD, Created in Your Love?

6.   My favorite watercolor is Janet Fish's Spring Party.

7.   Your Threa in your title is misspelled; it should be spelled Three.

8.   My mother enjoys the magazine, Arizona Foothills.

Rule 1: Use quotation marks (" ") to indicate someone's exact words.

"My pony's name is Trot," said Lizzy.

A. In a split quotation, place quotation marks around each part spoken.

"My answer," exclaimed Deca, "is right!"

B. In a split quotation, do not place the end quotation mark until the person has finished speaking.

"I'll phone Anna," said Lexi, "if you want. What is her number?"

🕉 *Periods and commas are placed inside quotation marks. Other punctuation is placed outside unless it is included in the actual quotation.*

Rule 2: Use quotation marks (" ") to enclose the title of short poems, short stories, nursery rhymes, songs, chapters, articles, and essays.

poem ~ "Hot Line"   chapter ~ "Bears"
short story ~ "My Funny Cat"   article ~ "Get a Life"
nursery rhyme ~ "Three Men in a Tub"   essay ~ "Mentoring"
song ~ "I've Been Working on the Railroad"

Easy Grammar **Note: Any *item* that is contained within a larger one is usually placed in quotation marks.** For example:
A chapter is within a book.

೪೬೪೬೪೬೪೬೪೬೪೬೪೬೪೬೪೬೪೬೪೬೪೬

Directions: Write a short title.

1. poem - _____   5. song - _____

2. short story - _____   6. article - _____

3. essay - _____   7. chapter - _____

4. nursery rhyme - _____

294

Rule 1: Use quotation marks (" ") to indicate someone's exact words.

"Where's Tessa?" asked Madison.

A. In a split quotation, place quotation marks around each part spoken.

"The little pinto," said Tom, "is my brother's horse."

B. In a split quotation, do not place the end quotation mark until the person has finished speaking.

"This hiking trail," said Parker, "looks good. Let's take it."

ॐ**Periods and commas are placed inside quotation marks. Other punctuation is placed outside unless it is included in the actual quotation.**

Rule 2: Use quotation marks (" ") to enclose the title of short poems, short stories, nursery rhymes, songs, chapters, articles, and essays.

article ~ "Amelia Island"   poem ~ "Yawning"
chapter ~ "Bears"   short story ~ "Sammy Goes Fishing"
essay ~ "The Civil War"   song ~ "I Dream of Jeanie"
nursery rhyme ~ "Three Blind Mice"

Easy Grammar Note: Any item that is contained within a larger one is usually placed in quotation marks. For example: A newspaper (large) contains many articles (small).

෴෴෴෴෴෴෴෴෴෴෴෴෴෴෴෴෴෴෴෴෴෴

Directions: Use quotation marks where needed.

1. Hannah asked, When will dinner be ready?

2. The song, Created by Your Love, was written by his mother.

3. Momma, I need you to help me, said the little girl.

4. Have you read the poem titled The Sugar Lady by Frank Asch?

5. Is Amelia Island, asked Peter, off the coast of Florida?

6. I like the nursery rhyme, Old King Cole.

Directions: Place quotation marks or underline the following titles.

1. a ship, Lusitania

2. a book, Daddy's Girl

3. a movie, Free Willy

4. a poem, Rhinos Purple, Hippos Green

5. an article, How to Paint Your Room

6. a magazine, Kids

7. a play, American Spy

8. a short story, Phoebe and the General

9. a song, Getting to Know You

10. an album, God Is Love

11. an airplane, Air Force 1

12. a newspaper, The Financial Times

13. a television show, Jeopardy

14. a chapter, Pronouns

15. a work of art, Wagon Boss

16. an essay, Comparing Plant Cells and Animal Cells

17. a train, James

18. a nursery rhyme, Baa, Baa, Black Sheep

19. a newspaper article, The Stock Market

A. Insert periods where needed.

1. I Mountains
      A Mt Hood
      B Mt Elden
  II Hills

2. Mr Contos now lives at 7252 N Dee Ave

3. On Mon , Aug 26, they'll fly to Denmark

ॐॐॐॐॐॐॐॐॐ

B. Insert commas where needed.

1. Emma do you want to make a snowman?

2. Your dog may go with us but your ferret needs to remain behind.

3. Her Victorian hat was decorated with three feathers lace and a large flower.

4. No the church bells have not rung.

5. The company address is P. O. Box 30012 Gettysburg PA 17325.

6. The United States declared its freedom on July 4 1776.

7. Dakota said "I need water for my hermit crab."

8. Kate and Becca his granddaughters went fishing with him.

9. Monday October 10 2005 was Canada's Thanksgiving Day.

10. Printz Dave L.

11. During the morning practice was held on the playground.

12. On January 1 2016 she will be sixteen.

13. "We must measure the width of this room " said the carpet installer.

C. Directions: Use a question mark or an exclamation point where needed.

1. Where is my yoga outfit

2. Ouch I hurt my toe

✺✺✺✺✺✺✺✺✺✺

D. Directions: Write the answer.

1. the contraction for **they are** - _____

2. the contraction for **I would** - _____

3. the contraction for **will not** - _____

4. balloons belonging to one girl - _____

5. balloons belonging to more than one girl - _____

6. balloons belonging to more than one child - _____

7. a barn for several horses - _____

✺✺✺✺✺✺✺✺✺✺

E. Directions: Place a colon or a semicolon where needed.

1. Our bus leaves at 3 45 this afternoon please be at the bus stop by then.

2. These items are missing from my drawer a pen, an eraser, and a ruler.

3. Things that begin with <u>H</u>
    -hamsters
    -habits
    -horses

4. Dear Ms. Listiack

✺✺✺✺✺✺✺✺✺✺

F. Directions: Place a hyphen where needed.

1. Divide *partner* into syllables: _____

2. Seventy four bubble wrapped teapots were unboxed.

298

G. Directions: Use underlining where needed.

1. Have you seen the movie, Mary Poppins, starring Julie Andrews?

2. Do you know about the airplane, Enola Gay?

3. You'll like the cookbook titled A Very Berry Cookbook.

4. Your p needs to be capitalized in the word, postmaster.

5. His aunt went on a cruise to Alaska on the Queen Star.

છ~છ~છ~છ~છ~છ~છ~છ~છ~છ

H. Directions: Use quotation marks where needed.

1. Joy asked, Did you fill the birdbath?

2. His favorite poem, The Midnight Ride of Paul Revere, tells a story.

3. Our friends have arrived, said Gretta.

4. Do you like the newspaper column titled Theft Reports each week?

છ~છ~છ~છ~છ~છ~છ~છ~છ~છ

I. Directions: Write the following.

1. Write the abbreviations for the days of the week.

a. Sunday – _____   e. Thursday – _____

b. Monday – _____   f. Friday – _____

c. Tuesday – _____   g. Saturday – _____

d. Wednesday – _____

2. Write the abbreviations for the months of the year.

a. January – _____   f. September – _____

b. February – _____   g. October – _____

c. March – _____   h. November – _____

d. April – _____   i. December – _____

e. August – _____

Directions: Insert needed punctuation.

1. No we havent learned French

2. Dear Sir

3. Has Capt Juan S Ramos visited Dans classroom

4.
                                    43 Briar Lane

                                    Terre Haute IN   47808

                                    July 4 2005

     Dear Liz

          Yes youre invited to our home at 12 W Maple Street Portland Maine

     Bring the following a sleeping bag a backpack and camping clothes My

     Dad will take us on an two day camping trip Wow I cant wait

                                    Your friend

                                    Tessa

5. Your t in torn isnt large enough Parker

6. I read the book titled Full Moon you would enjoy reading it

7. Austin said Many Japanese tourists visit the Grand Canyon

8. The two boys mother helped them to build a two wheeled cart

9. Mr and Mrs Fromm were married on Saturday Oct 8 2005

10. I should buy twenty two bottles of water but I dont have enough money

11. Their flight will depart at 2 30 for San Antonio Texas

WRITING

NOTES

An appositive is a word or phrase (group of words) that explains a noun.

Example: Spin**, their ferret,** is in a cage.

appositive

WITHOUT THE PHRASE, *THEIR FERRET*, WE WOULDN'T KNOW WHO SPIN IS!

An appositive is placed next to the word it explains.

Example: We saw Lou**, our postman,** today.

appositive

WITHOUT THE PHRASE, *OUR POSTMAN*, WE WOULDN'T KNOW WHO LOU IS!

An appositive is set off by commas.

Examples: Have you been to Denver**, the capital of Colorado**?

Miss Cook**, a nurse,** stopped to help.

દેવદેવદેવદેવદેવદેવદેવ

Directions: Place the appositive by the word it explains. Be sure to insert a comma or commas where needed.

Example: He gave me a gowan. A gowan is a white field flower.

____**He gave me a gowan**._____

____**He gave me a gowan,** *a white field flower*._____

1. We asked Jana and Jo to go to the lake with us. Jana and Jo are our classmates.

____**We asked Jana and Jo**_____

____**to go to the lake with us.**_____

2. Grandma served watermelon. Watermelon is my favorite food.

    Grandma served watermelon

3. They saw karos in New Zealand. Karos are small trees.

    They saw karos   **in New**

    Zealand.

4. Michael Jordan appeared on television. Michael is a basketball player.

    Michael Jordan

    appeared on television.

5. Are you attending the fiesta? It is Pablo's graduation party.

    Are you attending the fiesta

6. We watched a movie. It was a scary one that frightened us.

    We watched a movie

7. Tessa bought a kite. Tessa is Eddie's sister.

    Tessa   **bought a kite.**

8. She sold the Bar S. The Bar S is a ranch in eastern Montana.

    She sold the Bar S

An appositive is a word or phrase (group of words) that explains.

Example: Jacy**, their grandson,** is two months old.

appositive

WITHOUT THE PHRASE, *THEIR GRANDSON* , WE WOULDN'T KNOW WHO JACY IS!

An appositive is placed next to the word it explains.

Example: We studied amino acids**, building blocks of protein.**

appositive

BUILDING BLOCKS OF PROTEIN EXPLAINS AMINO ACIDS.

An appositive is set off by commas.

Examples: I like sushi**, a dish of rice and raw fish.**

This tine**, a prong on my fork,** is bent.

తతతతతతతతతతతత

Directions: Place the appositive by the word it explains. Be sure to insert a comma or commas where needed.

Example: Gertrude Ederle was the first woman to swim the English Channel. She was only nineteen.

___**Gertrude Ederle,** *the first woman to swim the*___

___*English Channel,* **was only nineteen.**___

1. Aren entered the hospital in a hurry. Aren is a doctor.

___**Aren,**_____**, entered the**___

___**hospital in a hurry.**_____

2. His aunt and uncle made sorbet. Sorbet is an Eastern sherbet.

   His aunt and uncle made sorbet, _____

   _____

3. Martha Jane Canary was once a scout for General Custer. She was also known as "Calamity Jane."

   Martha Jane Canary, _____ **,** _____

   was once a scout for General Custer. _____

4. Faith and Jenna are identical twins. They were born five minutes apart.

   Faith and Jenna, _____ **,** _____

   were born five minutes apart. _____

5. A set of George Washington's teeth is kept at Mount Vernon. Mount Vernon is Washington's home.

   A set of George Washington's teeth is kept at Mount _____

   Vernon, _____

6. Mr. London is a steel worker. Mr. London became our new mayor.

   Mr. London, _____ **, became** _____

   our new mayor. _____

7. Bill Robinson was a famous tap dancer in the 1930s. His nickname was "Bojangles."

   Bill Robinson, _____ **,** _____

   was nicknamed "Bojangles." _____

306

An appositive is a word or phrase (group of words) that explains a noun. An appositive is placed next to the word it explains.

> Example: Sara, **my cousin**, will arrive tomorrow.
> **appositive**

An appositive is set off by a comma or commas.

> Example: That glass**, an old goblet,** was given to my mother.
> **appositive**

ॐॐॐॐॐॐॐॐॐॐ

Directions: Write a sentence using an appositive.

Example: Emma talked with his mother. Emma is his karate instructor.

Emma, his karate instructor, talked with his mother.

1. Jack gave a speech. Jack is our class president.

    _____

2. The artist painted a picture of a bobolink. A bobolink is a songbird.

    _____

    _____

3. The winners were Mika and Rob. They received tickets to a concert.

    _____

    _____

4. Have you been to Sicily? Sicily is an island at the tip of Italy.

    _____

    _____

5. Flummery is good. Flummery is a dish made of boiled wheatmeal.

    _____

    _____

An appositive is a word or phrase (group of words) that explains a noun. An appositive is placed next to the word it explains.

Example: Lisa gave him a present, **a blue-striped shirt**.
appositive

An appositive is set off by a comma or commas.

Example: Kasha**, a fabric made from wool and hair,** is soft.
appositive

ৰ৵ৰ৵ৰ৵ৰ৵ৰ৵ৰ৵ৰ৵ৰ৵ৰ৵ৰ৵ৰ৵

Directions: Write a sentence using an appositive.

Example: Do you like gumbo? Gumbo is a spicy soup thickened with okra.

Do you like gumbo, a spicy soup thickened with okra?

1.   The new puppy fell over his dish and spilled his water. The new puppy
     is a white furry husky.

     _____

     _____

2.   Paul is driving his new vehicle. His new vehicle is a red tractor-trailer.

     _____

     _____

3.   They used Masonite for their science project. Masonite is fiberboard
     made from wood fiber.

     _____

     _____

4.   We visited a kraal in Africa. A kraal is a village surrounded by a fence.

     _____

     _____

A **semicolon** is a comma with a period above it **(;)**.

A semicolon may be used to join two complete thoughts. That means that each thought must be able to stand alone as a **complete sentence**.

It's important to know if the group of words expresses a complete thought.

Examples: Your hairbrush is on the floor.   (**complete thought**)
                                                                              (**sentence**)

Walked her dog.   (**not a complete thought**)
Where's the subject? We don't know *who* walked her dog.

After we went to our game. (**not a complete thought**)

The sentence contains a **subject** (we) and a **verb** (went), but it does not express a complete thought. If you said to a friend, "After we went to our game," and walked away, your friend would have no idea what you are trying to tell him.

ം ം ം ം ം ം ം ം ം ം ം ം

Directions: Write **S** in the blank if the group of words is a sentence (complete thought). Write **NS** in the blank if the group of words is not a sentence (not a complete thought).

1. _____   Lucy rides her horse bareback.

2. _____   A new pope had been chosen.

3. _____   Beginning to rain.

4. _____   When you are finished.

5. _____   Mark was hired as a waiter.

6. _____   Has a cat scratched your arm?

7. _____   Sent on an errand for ten minutes.

8. _____   After a roofer started a drill.

9. _____   Your idea funny.

10. _____   Jan wants a purple coat.

A **semicolon** is a comma with a period above it **(;)**.

A semicolon may be used to join two complete thoughts. That means that each thought must be able to stand alone as a **complete sentence**.

It's important to know if the group of words expresses a complete thought.

> Examples: The car's fender is damaged.   (**complete thought**)
>   (**sentence**)
>
> Susan in the pink sweater.   (**not a complete thought**)
> Where's the verb?
>
> If I earn a few dollars. (**not a complete thought**)

The sentence contains a *subject* (I) and a *verb* (earn), but it does not express a complete thought.

৵৵৵৵৵৵৵৵৵৵৵৵৵

Directions: Write **S** in the blank if the group of words is a sentence (complete thought). Write **NS** in the blank if the group of words is not a sentence (not a complete thought).

1. _____   The landed in the bushes.
2. _____   Before she prepared food for a picnic.
3. _____   Breaking away and suddenly yelling.
4. _____   She worked on a scrapbook.
5. _____   This limited to four people.
6. _____   Many people have visited the Alamo.
7. _____   A fire in the fireplace.
8. _____   That little girl speaks Spanish.
9. _____   They to a horse show last weekend.
10. _____   Having eaten at a local restaurant.

Name_____

Date_____

A semicolon is a comma with a period above it (;). It joins two complete thoughts.

    1st complete thought (sentence):   This lettuce has turned brown.
    2nd complete thought (sentence):   I'll have to throw it away.

Example: This lettuce has turned brown; I'll have to throw it away.

The two thoughts must be about the same topic!

    Wrong: My sister lives in Alaska; I'm having steak for dinner.

    Right: My sister lives in Alaska; I'm visiting her this summer.

Sometimes, words such as *however* or *therefore* will follow the semicolon. Place a comma after *however* or *therefore.*

    Example: I like fish; ***however,*** I don't like fish tacos.
    ᝌᝌᝌᝌᝌᝌᝌᝌᝌᝌᝌᝌ

Directions: Use a semicolon where needed.

1. Kim is in first grade he is already reading.

2. Stop the bus I want to get off.

3. Tessa has a sore throat therefore, she didn't sing.

4. Their car is old however, it runs very well.

5. She models for a designer her picture appeared in *Fashion Q.*

6. Mom didn't fish however, she sat by the creek and read a book.

7. Cody is taking college classes he wants to be a history teacher.

8. I like baked yams they're one of my favorite foods.

9. Tate entered church therefore, he turned his cell phone off.

Name_____

WRITING SENTENCES

Date_____

Using Semicolons

A semicolon is a comma with a period above it (;). It joins two complete thoughts. The two thoughts must be about the <u>same</u> topic!

Sometimes, words such as *however* or *therefore* will follow the semicolon. Place a comma after *however* or *therefore*.

      Example: His arm is in a cast; ***however***, he climbed over the fence.

                ॐॐॐॐॐॐॐॐॐॐॐॐ

Directions: The first complete thought has been written for you. Place a semicolon and finish the sentence.

<u>Remember</u>: **You can use *however* or *therefore* if it makes sense. Don't forget the comma after these words.**

1. <u>It has stopped raining</u>_____

    _____

2. <u>My friend twisted his ankle</u>_____

    _____

3. <u>Carla made blueberry tarts</u>_____

    _____

4. <u>The dusty road has many potholes</u>_____

    _____

5. <u>We have been assigned a social studies project</u>_____

    _____

A semicolon is a comma with a period above it (;). It joins two complete thoughts.   The two thoughts must be about the <u>same</u> topic!

Sometimes, words such as *however* or *therefore* will follow the semicolon. Place a comma after *however* or *therefore.*

> Example: His arm is in a cast; ***however,*** he climbed over the fence.

> ରେଶରେଶରେଶରେଶରେଶରେଶରେଶ

Directions: The first complete thought has been written for you. Place a semicolon and finish the sentence.

<u>Remember</u>: **You can use *however* or *therefore* if it makes sense. Don't forget the**

> **comma after these words.**

1. <u>Kim will be attending a job fair this week</u> _____

_____

2. <u>The car salesman showed the couple a car</u> _____

_____

3. <u>Patty has joined the band</u> _____

_____

4. <u>The child made a funny face</u> _____

_____

5. <u>The students like to write</u> _____

_____

In order to understand compound sentences, we need to review *complete thoughts*.

> Examples: Mary likes math.   (**complete thought**)

> While Toya was on vacation. (**not a complete thought**)

The sentence contains a ***subject*** (<u>Toya</u>) and a ***verb*** (<u>was</u>), but it does not express a complete thought. More information is needed.

A compound sentence is formed by joining **two complete thoughts** with ***and***, ***but***, or ***or***.

> Their dad is a baker, ***and*** his mother is a teacher.

> **complete thought**   **complete thought**

> Granddad is an artist, ***but*** he doesn't sell his works.

> **complete thought**   **complete thought**

🙥🙥🙥🙥🙥🙥🙥🙥🙥🙥🙥

Directions: Write **<u>S</u>** in the blank if the group of words is a sentence (complete thought). Write **<u>NS</u>** in the blank if the group of words is not a sentence (not a complete thought).

1. _____   When he signed his name.

2. _____   The company's president called a meeting.

3. _____   Before he sat at his computer.

4. _____   The baby will be christened on Sunday.

5. _____   Although we left for the party early.

6. _____   Whenever the toddler becomes angry.

7. _____   Grandma won a 5k race.

8. _____   After the last inning of the game.

9. _____   Mario's grades are always good.

Name_____   **Writing Compound**

Date_____   **Sentences**

A compound sentence is formed by joining **two complete thoughts** with
and, ***but***, or ***or***.

They may board their dog**,** ***or*** they might have to take him along.

complete thought   **complete thought**

We placed strings of lights on our house**,** ***but*** they wouldn't blink.

complete thought   **complete thought**

Place a comma before a conjunction when it is joining two complete thoughts.

A pinto can be a type of horse**,** **but** it can also be a type of bean.

৵৵৵৵৵৵৵৵৵৵৵

Directions: Circle each complete thought. Place a comma where needed.

1.   His sister is a gymnast but she only practices once a week.

2.   You may hand your paper to your friend or you may place it in my basket.

3.   They are going to Tulsa next year and I'll meet them there.

4.   Joan goes to bed early but she doesn't like to get up in the morning.

5.   The bus must be on time or we will be late for school.

6.   The Cherry Creek Arts Festival will be next week but I can't attend.

7.   An Airedale is a terrier and it has a short, dense coat.

8.   He has read several mysteries but he hasn't read a biography.

9.   Grandpa makes us breakfast on Mondays or he takes us to a café.

10.   Our family went to the zoo, but I didn't see any zebras.

A compound sentence is formed by joining **two complete thoughts** with **and**, **but**, or **or**.

Place a **comma before a conjunction** when it is joining two complete thoughts.

Example: Royce wrote a poem, but he didn't share it.
                 complete thought   complete thought

ৰ৵ৰ৵ৰ৵ৰ৵ৰ৵ৰ৵ৰ৵ৰ৵ৰ৵ৰ৵ৰ৵ৰ৵

Directions: Write a conjunction and another complete thought to finish each compound sentence. Be sure to place a comma before the conjunction.

1. My uncle was born in North Dakota _____

_____

2. You may sit at this table _____

_____

3. Chessa painted her bedroom purple _____

_____

4. Grandma bought stock last year _____

_____

5. Don wants to go to a dude ranch in Arizona _____

_____

6. An usher asked Lalah to sit down _____

_____

Name_____   **Writing Compound**

Date_____   **Sentences**

A compound sentence is formed by joining **two complete thoughts** with

and, **but**, or **or**. Place a **comma before the conjunction**.

Example: Our team scored the final goal, but we lost the game.
complete thought   **complete thought**

ಶಿ ಶಿ ಶಿ ಶಿ ಶಿ ಶಿ ಶಿ ಶಿ ಶಿ ಶಿ ಶಿ

Directions: Write a conjunction and another complete thought to finish each
compound sentence.

1. The man demanded his money back _____

_____

2. Their class visited a television station _____

_____

3. Pedro may take his daughter horseback riding _____

_____

4. An author signed books at a local bookstore _____

_____

5. They are having a cookout _____

_____

6. Snow drifted onto the road _____

_____

7. James is going to New York City on business _____

_____

INDEX